Sexual Healing

spiritconnect

connecting releasing resourcing

Hi Daryl,

I promised to get you a copy of Gerald's
book ages ago! Here it is — with compliments
Good to see you both on Thursday!

[signature]

churches, teams and ministries working together for local and global transformation - 'rediscovering the church as a living reflection of jesus'

john & christine noble 1 the knoll leatherhead surrey kt22 8xh
website: www.spiritconnect.org email: office@spiritconnect.org fax: (0)1372 373233
registered charity number 1096236 part of the pioneer network

SEXUAL HEALING

Identity – Sexuality – Calling

Gerald Coates and Nathan Ferreira

New Wine Press

New Wine Press
An imprint of RoperPenberthy Publishing Ltd
Springfield House
23 Oatlands Drive
Weybridge
Surrey KT13 9LZ
UK

ISBN 978-1-905991-82-2

Typeset by Avocet Typeset, Chilton, Aylesbury, Bucks
Cover design by CCD, www.ccdgroup.co.uk
Printed in the UK

CONTENTS

Acknowledgements

Nathan Ferreira

Abba, I am yours. Thank you for reconciling my life. For breathing life into the words I say and the things I do. It is all for your glory.

Jonathan Logan, after God, you first saw what I couldn't see; your initial mentoring really shaped the person I wanted to be and I will be forever grateful for the challenge you gave to be a disciple of Christ.

Oscar Hyde and family, you continue to teach me how to love like Christ loves me, by showing me Christ's love every time I see you.

Luke Haley and family, I hope you will continue to expose my weaknesses as a fallen human being and that we will carry on laughing off all unnecessary seriousness well into our old age together.

Sam Harding, not only are you, like me, assistant to Gerald, but you have become a brother in Christ. I will always learn from your humility and strength of identity in Him, and I am blessed to have you as a part of my life.

Gerald, thank you for your obedience to Christ. You have inspired, challenged and helped transform my life. Thank you for seeing what so many others had seen and acting on it. Thank you for asking me The Question!

Ashlee, for over six years you have been a continual reflection of God's love, mercy and grace in my life. I pray that I can do the same. You inspire me to show others the love of God that you have shown me.

Dad, Mum, Hannah and Sophie, you will always be my best friends – who challenge, inspire, motivate and annoy me! You have always been a safety net of God's grace in my life. I love you all so much and I am so grateful that I will always have your prayers, encouragement and love. I look forward to spending the rest of my life in your company.

Thank you also to Ollie Evans, Gary Ward, Dr Gareth Jones, Dr Mike Viccary, Samuel Lee, Cathy Nobles, John and Val Peacock, and all the friends, mentors, family and teachers who have been examples of Christ and shaped me to be the man I am today.

Acknowledgements

Gerald Coates

Holy Spirit, you continually guide me into truth, despite my distractions. Thank you for ensuring that we have not been left a confusing or unintelligible series of documents teaching us how to live and relate to one another.

Nathan, as well you know this book would never have seen the light of day, were it not for The Question and your initial spluttering response! Yes we laugh at it all now, but it remains a privilege for me to work with you in this and other projects. Words are not enough.

Anona – without you where would I be today? Our 46 years of marriage have made me a better, more whole and humorous person – mainly because of you. Thank you for trusting me to work on this book, without finding myself in trouble – your trust has strengthened me.

Caleb Meakins, Ben Cooper, Ben John, Joshua George and William, thank you for being so willing to share your important stories of hope – we will see some of you on the tour! And Sam, thanks for putting up with an office that for weeks seemed only concerned with addiction, deviation and the language of sex! But you have been privileged to hear the wonderful stories of breakthrough. You are a great person and personal assistant. It is such a privilege to work with you.

Richard and RoperPenberthy Publishing; for trusting us to be specific without being graphic. We have felt let down by others with their broad generalisations but you have taken risks with us that we are sure will give practical help to bless guys everywhere!

And finally Timothy Keller – we have never met but your writings have blessed, nourished and strengthened me. The chapter on M near the close of the book should really have your name on it – but I am not quite that humble! I have met and been privileged to prophesy over Royalty, Downing Street office holders, global entertainers and brilliant international Christian leaders – and loads of nameless, faceless people (well at least up until now!) but would *really* like to meet you and thank you! I sincerely hope I will one day!

Introduction

Gerald Coates

The Creator seems to have such an amazing soft spot for us humans!

This despite the fact we are all wrong doers – who do damage to ourselves and others, as well as the earth on which we exist. We do this by living selfishly, defensively and irresponsibly, for impure pleasure, control and personal satisfaction. This can last for 60 seconds, 60 minutes or 60 years!

You've only got to take a look at so-called biblical heroes to see what an absolute mess they sometimes got into! And this is particularly true in the area of sexuality. Sex was, and is today, mostly done in private, as the majority of us are not daft enough to sin too much in public! No, we save this kind of behaviour for behind closed – and sometimes locked – doors.

As it happens, those with some sort of faith tend to have a greater sensitivity to sexual wrongdoing. (This includes self-indulgent damage, such as building up a mental library of countless images to be drawn upon day and night.) Conflict emerges when conscience, morals informed by good influences, scripture and the Holy Spirit collide with images and compulsive behaviour. This mix hinders us from being the very best we can be for God. Disillusionment with ourselves, regularly failing and apologising, promising 'not to do it again' leads us down a weary road that results in cover-ups, mediocrity and depression.

This damage and wrongdoing disconnects us from heaven. Some readers may feel that they have never, ever connected to such a place or dimension! But why bother? We are, after all, living on just one of billions of stars and planets in our galaxy and this is merely one of billions of galaxies in the known universe. Who are we? Do we matter? Well history and, for Nathan, myself and many others, experience tells us that something was done that would give us back our identity, shape and inform our sexuality and call us on to higher and better things.

This book has been written for those who want to discover, or rediscover, who they are, what to do with their sexuality pre- and even post marriage (allowing that many will remain single) and how to develop day-to-day spirituality in concrete, effective and tangible ways. Those who know who they are tend to get more done.

A sex-soaked culture

Today sex is everywhere. It is inescapable. It is in the lyrics of globally sung songs, in barely dressed models in advertisements, in popular music videos, glossy magazines and especially in certain Sunday and even weekday newspapers. Raunchy images are displayed on shelves and in racks, which young children can easily view. You can even purchase a local village newspaper and respond to advertisements promising you the pleasures of being wanked off (sorry I didn't prepare you for that one!) – oral, gay and full sex – but for a fee of course! Stand-up comedians use sex, sometimes humorously but usually with vulgarity and coarseness – two words we hear little of, as our culture has become so swiftly debased.

But as we all know, the biggie, the real biggie, is available, affordable and anonymous. It is on your desk, in your bedroom, on your travels and ends up in your head, bed and bathroom. It is, of course, internet pornography. I read in a national newspaper, that in a recent survey in Australia 25 percent of men (not committed Christian men) are deeply concerned with how much internet pornography they are watching and using.

The Sex Atlas recorded that there are on average 68 million pornographic searches daily[1] and this represents a staggering 25 percent of all online searches.

So what is normal?

One of the problems in today's culture, is that no one knows what is normal anymore. Compared to the current tsunami of non-relational sex, virtual ignorance about sexuality, when I was only a few years younger than Nathan's age, was bliss! Now who is doing what with whom can be read about in *Hello!* or *OK* magazines, in regular newspapers and seen or heard in occasional news bulletins. And it would not be an exaggeration to say that the more money the famous and wealthy spend on their wedding day the sooner the likelihood of divorce occurs. But what about *normal* people? What should we be genuinely concerned with and why? After all, there is so much greater evil in the world than our sex lives...

For Nathan, his journey of identity confusion, teenage sexual pleasure, God, spirituality and his future started with inquisitiveness and (as you are about to read), with the mild pleasures of occasional internet porn. It finished with a young man swiftly demoralised, living two lives barely on a nodding acquaintance with one another and desperately looking for a way out! It can – so easily – become an addiction, carried over to affect girlfriends, marriage, (yes marriage) work and even church. A surprisingly high level of pornography is accessed between 9am–5pm Monday to Friday – in the workplace! Using salaried time for Facebook or porn can be a sackable offence so why do people still do it?

However our sexuality is not simple – it is complex. Most of us need help and understanding as well as other people's stories of overcoming such dark places and the promise of hope for a better future. These next few chapters aim to do just that.

And let me tell you as someone over four decades older than Nathan, one's sexuality doesn't evaporate with old age. There is a story about an elderly wife asking her husband, 'Shall we go upstairs and be intimate?' He is reported to have responded, 'I can do one or the other but I can't do both!'

Our bodies may eventually hinder us from some expressions of active sexual pleasure, but that only makes the allure of non-relational, minimally active internet porn so attractive.

However, Nathan and I have never intended that this book you are now reading to simply be about past sexual failures and hoped for future freedom and deliverance. There are much bigger issues at stake here. Nathan has most of his adult life ahead of him. I, on the other hand, am living in the last quarter of my life here on planet earth. But for both of us, God has placed big issues on our hearts and minds – for you.

So what are the big issues?

Put simply, our main concern is how can we help develop strong, reliable, fun-filled, honest, biblically informed men of character and calling in such a disintegrating sexual culture? We cannot teach men to accept pornography and subsequent behaviour as normal, because 'everyone is doing it'. This abandons guys to cover-ups, lies, embarrassment and shame.

Instead we want to produce disciples of Christ – and a disciple is someone who takes another as his teacher or model. 'Be imitators of me, just as I also am of Christ' wrote the first century disciple of Christ, Saul who became Paul.[2] What an amazingly different world it would be, if we all lived as Christ! He was culturally relevant when He lived on earth, yet so different. The difference was what was so attractive to His followers – His disciples.

Being culturally relevant is not the same as gradually becoming like the culture around us, until we are unrecognisable from the rest of the world. Bill Johnson, an American preacher of note, has said that being culturally relevant is living, in relationship with others, a life much of the rest of society aspires to and hopes for. I suggest that all of society would aspire to love and forgiveness in relationships, faithfulness and commitment, safety for the vulnerable and young, happiness, relational care, sacrificial provision, security and honesty about failure and even wrongdoing. These are the things most of us aspire to, even though we may fail. Christ's disciples live in the dimension of heaven but on the earth – that's called the Kingdom of God – and are focused on the Christian community – the Church! And church is not a special meeting in a special building, but a 24-hour, seven day a week lifestyle. It includes gatherings because people who love each other want to gather around the things that affect others. This includes sung worship to the living God, prayer for our world, (local and international) and of course the greatest shaper of it all – the teaching of scripture.

So here we go!

Take a journey through these chapters. Your small but important story, along with millions of others, keeps the big story of God at work in His world – alive and relevant. We pray it will help you rediscover identity, manage your sexuality and fulfil your calling, in household, education, workplace, ministry and the wider world we are all a part of.

And remember – *success is the ability to survive failure!*

Gerald Coates,
Great Bookham, Leatherhead,
October 2012

Notes

1. Haeberle, Erwin J and Sutton, Laird, *The Sex Atlas*, Continuum Publishing.
2. 1 Corinthians 11:1, NASV.

Credentials

Gerald Coates has been married to author, interior designer and homemaker Anona for 46 years. They have three sons, two daughters-in-law and three grandchildren. They live in a town called Hope – sometimes called Leatherhead – in Surrey, the last place Wesley preached – in 1791.

Gerald had an average education, but became deputy head boy in nearby Cobham, Surrey. He then attended Epsom and Ewell Art School and entered into the world of display advertising, exhibition and design.

He gave his life to Christ at a youth camp when almost 12 years of age. At 17 years he was in a motorcycle crash (no one else was involved) and was given four hours to live. Britain's then best-known racing driver, Stirling Moss, also crashed that day, 12 May 1962, which finished his career. They both ended up in the same top brain hospital, Atkinson Morley, in Wimbledon, southwest London.

After recovery Gerald joined the only evangelical church in Cobham, which was anti-pentecostal/charismatic. This became a problem because, keen to know more of God, he prayed to be filled with the Spirit and, one day, began to sing in another language – tongues (a phenomenon he had never heard) while cycling. As a result he was obliged to leave the church with several others. He began Cobham Christian Fellowship, one of the earliest churches in the House Church Movement, which is now called the New Church Movement – a phrase he invented, according to Dr Andrew Walker, author of *Restoring the Kingdom*. 'The only book worth reading on the movement', Gerald comments!

The church became known as Pioneer People, which spawned the Pioneer network of churches in the UK and overseas. Well known people in the Pioneer network included the worship band *Delirious?*, author and communicator Jeff Lucas, worship leaders Noel Richards, Dave Bilbrough and Sue Rinaldi, children's author and recording artist Ishmael and John and Christine Noble, both speakers and writers. Partnerships with March for Jesus, the Aids initiative ACET, the student ministry Fusion, the 24/7 prayer network led by Pete Grieg and DNA, the training course led by Pete Gilbert, have been important ministries.

Today Gerald is leading a newish church in Leatherhead, Surrey – Pioneer Engage. He chairs an evangelical charismatic round table (The Waverley Forum), and is one of two ambassadors and a patron for Monkton Combe School in Bath. He is pastor to the Gulu Mission Initiative, Uganda where he regularly travels to. He has taken part in numerous television and radio programmes on BBC TV, ITV, BBC Radio 2, 4 and 5 as well as being featured in articles in the *Mail on Sunday* colour supplement, *The Sunday Times* colour supplement, several national newspapers and countless Christian magazines, TV and radio programmes. He is best known as a speaker and writer of nine books, though this is his first in over 15 years!

He has told his wife, Anona, he would like his tombstone to read: 'By God's grace we changed the heart and face of the Church in the UK'.

Introduction

Nathan Ferreira

So what does a 21-year-old bring to this publication that Gerald has not already covered? It is true that Gerald has a wealth of experience and pastoral care, but I had to grow up and deal with things in a completely different world from him – so I am telling things from my perspective.

Our world today is a world of targets and goals, ambition and desires. Targets we fail to hit, goals we fail to meet. Ambitions we can never achieve and desires that lead us to form a negative self-image. Too often we are weighed down, corrupted and restrained by our mistakes. These mistakes prevent us from seeing and living out who we truly are. For so many people these mistakes are rarely brought to light; they are hidden away, too shameful to admit.

In Christian circles sexual sin can be perceived as the 'worst sin' of all. The word 'sex' itself is often surrounded by coded language and harsh conviction. It is rarely confronted head on with the honesty, openness and language that is needed to help an increasing majority of young Christian men enter into freedom from the torturous situation that, like so many others, I once found myself in.

I was battling against a self-destructive cycle, yearning for the glamorous perfection that seemed abundant among other Christians. I was split down the middle. On one hand there was Nathan the upcoming leader, the one with a great heart for God and a great reputation within church, school and friends. Part of the seemingly perfect Ferreira family. This Nathan wanted to do something great for God. He was described as an exemplification of Christian morality, repeatedly told that indeed he would do 'great things'. However behind the masquerade of this Nathan was the other – a struggling child, fighting to keep the act up while trying to free himself from the weight of guilt and shame.

Identity crisis

The other Nathan was not worthy of any greatness, and certainly not capable of achieving any of the God-given dreams he may have had. He was struggling to understand who he was, never mind what he could do. This was all at a time in life when the world seemed to compete against him for the best university, job and girlfriend. He was trying to fight for a good relationship with God as well as everything else. This other Nathan was literally sick with anxiety and dangerously self-destructive. He had a worldview that was clouded by his sin. He struggled to see himself and others in the true light. His sin was the foundation of who he was.

As a Christian, the struggles that come with sex are complex and intertwined. They cannot be separated and dealt with as an isolated part of our anatomy. Corruption of sex is like a malignant tumour. It does not simply affect one area of our lives; it spreads with little or no control to other places too. As Christians trying to help those suffering we cannot just rip the problem out. Sexual sin leaves traces of its influence in all manner of places.

The original intention of sex is amazing. It is important and vital, like the initial healthy dividing cells whose corruption causes cancer. Gerald mentioned that we live in a sex-soaked culture and this can be carcinogenic to our lives.

Thank God it doesn't need to be fatal. There really is freedom, life, joy, peace, healing and love through one name alone. That is, Jesus Christ the Son of God who gave us the ministry of reconciliation, so that we can come to Him free from habitual, addictive behaviour and enter into a loving, relationship with Father God. So how can we have that? It is more than merely a 'sinners' prayer'.

I was a believer from an early age. I knew God, I called

myself a Christian. However I struggled to receive the freedom that everyone spoke about, and the overwhelming love that people, including me, would sing about. I knew the Light of the world, but my world was not light. There are so many ways that the Bible tells us we can receive freedom and life. I knew these verses; I knew my Bible too! Why then did it not 'work' for me? I had been on countless websites and watched numerous videos on how to be free. What was I missing?

Non-affecting truth

I was stuck in a world where the truth was not affecting my life and mind-set. An unbeliever can read the Bible, which is the truth, and not be set free. So is the scripture false? Of course not, but it is the application, acceptance and outworking of that truth where the challenge lies.

Gerald brings a vast array of experience and a large wealth of knowledge to this book. He has worked with many young people like myself but did not grow up in the same situation and world that I have. Within what I write I hope that I can provide support and guidance on the application and outworking of Gerald's experience and wisdom, bringing it into a modern context as well as contributing what I have learnt through my own conflicts.

We hope that we can help you to apply the truths of God to your own life and lifestyle. We are not writing simply to give you strength; tips to beat the system you find yourself in or to fight against the dark side of your self. We hope rather that as you read we can help you transform the way you think and live so that you can be healed, reconnect to heaven and realign yourself with the purpose God has intended for your life.

'What the mind dwells upon the body acts upon.'
Denis Waitley

Nathan Ferreira,
Great Bookham, Leatherhead,
October 2012

Credentials

Nathan was born on the 25 April 1992 in Trinidad. He grew up with a love for the outdoors, particularly the beach, the rainforest and all the life that comes with it. He attended Bishop Anstey Junior School from the age of four to ten before moving to Bradford, England with his family; mother Wendy, father Nigel and sisters Hannah and Sophie.

Nathan completed the rest of his primary education in England before attending Bradford Christian School from age 12 to 16. That is where he had his first exposure to international mission, going to Romania in 2006 and then India in 2008. This lit a real passion within his already growing Christian faith, which was fuelled also by mentors, involvement with various programmes and eventually a diploma in Christian thinking after his GCSEs were completed.

He left his primary school in Bradford school with good grades and secured a place in Bingley Grammar School. However he struggled with the workload, feeling a lack of purpose and wondering where his life was heading. Eventually this led to him to drop out in the early stages of 2010. Nathan believed a culinary route would be better and taught himself to cook. This was not to be the case – though the lessons he learnt and strong affinity with food continually pays off! Instead of pursuing the culinary arts Nathan re-familiarised himself with Youth With A Mission (YWAM), having gone to a Kings Kids Camp at an early age in Trinidad and having family connections with the organisation.

He decided in this stage of uncertainty that a Discipleship Training School (DTS) with YWAM would be the best route to take, as he had found fulfilment with the missions' trips at secondary school. He attended the justice-focused DTS in

Barbados and went to Haiti and the Dominican Republic on outreach with a team of 18. This was an extremely impactful time, which also included YWAM's 50th anniversary celebration. He then enquired about the next steps he felt he was to take: The School of Reconciliation and Justice (SORJ) with YWAM Harpenden.

The SORJ was a greatly fulfilling experience for Nathan, teaching more about the topics that had so captivated his heart from an early age. It was a place of blessing and he really enjoyed his time there regardless of the underlying issues.

That bubble was soon to burst, though, as he landed back in Bradford and found it incredibly hard to adapt back to normality. He eventually did but had very confused thoughts on what to do next and whether the passions and the things he cared about most deeply could ever come to the forefront of his life. He hit a brick wall, as doors closed on him from all angles. He felt unqualified and unable to live out the things that were on his heart. Emotionally down, he felt he had to confront some severe long-standing 'guy issues' that were progressively getting worse. Although surrounded by loving family and many friends who would have understood his predicament, these areas remained locked up inside his heart and mind. He fought back the best he could and found a great place in The Light Church where he was asked to become catering manager for the Bradford Food Bank. He thoroughly enjoyed this role and worked it alongside gathering young people from varied denominations in Bradford to create and engage in practical ministry opportunities.

Unexpectedly he received some words of encouragement from someone he had never heard of. To the writer they were simply words of comfort but, coming at the time they did, to Nathan they were prophetic. They were like an arrow to his heart. A close friend in Australia encouraged Nathan to make a new start and contact the writer. This resulted in several lengthy phonecalls, a weekend visit and the first, serious discussion about these personal, embarrassing issues he had ever had with anyone. A series of amazing incidents and choices were to turn Nathan's deep conflicts into a victorious celebration. This unintended journey resulted in Nathan sensing he may need a new start in a new situation. This is where he currently is, developing a portfolio of subjects to take into schools, and offering support and understanding to various youth initiatives.

This book is the first tangible result of his journey.

Guest Introduction: 'Last Man Standing'

Caleb Meakins

For me it starts with my family. I've a wonderful mother who has faithfully guided our family in the ways of God. She has such a passionate heart to seek His will that it becomes infectious to others around her. However we don't inherit the Kingdom of God through the deeds of the faithful parent. My own path has been full of potholes and peaks. It was through one of my biggest struggles that God really broke through to reveal Himself in such a powerful way.

My mountain is one that I'm sure the majority of males (and females) have stared at with defiance only to succumb to its towering intimidation. My mountain was lust. It truly started when I was 12 years old, the first time I was exposed to pornography. I was playing football with a group of friends when we stumbled across an X-rated VHS tape in amongst a pile of dead leaves. What I viewed shocked, enticed and perplexed me. The door was open to a world of self-gratification and addiction. As the years went by, and dial up turned to broadband, my habit became an addiction, which was putting stumbling blocks between God and me. Furthermore, I felt that I was the only one wrapped up in this messy sin and, with every indulgence, it was crippling my sense of identity. What had I become? What would people think if they knew the things that I thought, watched and did?

At the age of 16 I felt so hollow; my faith had taken a battering. But God doesn't give up on us so easily. That summer I attended a camp with my cousins over in America and that is where God began my journey of freedom. The young male leaders at the camp took all the lads aside and shared with us the struggles they'd had with lust, porn and masturbation. I remember looking at my cousin hoping he hadn't noticed I was sweating profusely from the conviction in my heart. I returned home from that camp and deleted every bit of filth I possessed.

I did not open my mouth once to share my struggles at that camp. Yet simply being in the presence of those opening up to share their journey and battle with porn, and seeing their break through with Jesus, released great freedom in me. On my return, my faith had received an injection of life. The grace and mercy that Jesus Christ poured out upon me was revealed. Christ had paid the price.

This change in me was something that I wanted to sustain. From the camp I learnt that opening up a dialogue with other Christian guys was key to shining a light on sin that thrives in the secrecy of darkness. So we did just that. In my small group of friends, we began to share each other's struggles, discovering we were all in the same broken boat. Little did we know that God was about to use the vulnerability that we so openly displayed amongst this group of young men. As we went our separate ways, some of us to study and others of us to work, we set ourselves a challenge to go for as long as we could without 'having a wank'. We created a secret Facebook group and titled it 'Last Man Standing' and on Jan 2010 the competition began. The rest, as they say, is history.

The Facebook group, initially created to track the competition, rapidly grew into a support network that highlighted the fact that this journey was very little about competition and everything to do with brotherhood and accountability. From this place the tag line 'Promoting Purity & Integrity' was birthed. The first year saw the group grow to 200 members. As the group grew organically we established some structure to the online network in the form of three goals. These included: 1) encouraging face-to-face accountability; 2) praying weekly – every Thursday we pray for ourselves, our churches and our nation, that the veil of addiction would be lifted and 3) use the group to encourage and build up each other while sharing our struggles so we can pray for each other and grow.

It is now 2013 and the Facebook group has almost 2,000 members. We have established groups in over 20 universities around the UK and a handful abroad. We have conducted several conferences and God is still doing an incredible work through it. I couldn't really tell you what the future holds for this network, as is evident from the journey of the group. We couldn't have predicted it would do what it does now. But, just as we stumbled into where we are now, we trust God will let us stumble into the place we are meant to be next.

We have learnt so many lessons from the group and our journey outside of it. But what has stood out the most is that this journey is not meant to be carried out alone. Firstly, God is here to walk alongside us. Secondly, God gave us each other to build relationships with and point to Him. It's in these relationships that we are reminded of God's love for us, the grace He pours out upon us and His desire to be in relationship with us. I hope by reading this book you may find yourself understanding this grace all the more, leading you to a place of finding tremendous freedom in Christ.

God didn't create us to be slaves to the secret sins that weigh us down, pulling us further away from His presence. We were made for more than this. God is greater than the trials that we face and it's through His strength that we find victory.

After all, no man stands who does not stand with Christ!

Caleb Meakins,
January 2013

Chapter 1

When I First Discovered

Nathan: I thoroughly enjoyed my childhood, which was full of adventure, fun and blessings. It provided me with many happy memories growing up in a loving, safe family. There was no specific reason that could be seen to produce problems later on in my youth. The root cause of what I would face was not my upbringing or family. My family loved me, and I them. They raised me with a strong faith, in a Spirit filled-church, in which I was used to being prophesied over and speaking in tongues from an early age. I knew my Bible and read it often as a child. I was being nurtured to do well in school, respect my elders and love God. I had a strong foundation, repeated comments of 'they're growing up so well' stick out in my mind. I was not set up to fail.

My parents told me about sex at a young age when I asked them some questions that were raised after a classmate told me how she walked in on her parents. But, even though I knew about sex, I was far more interested in climbing trees than anything else! It was only when I had moved to England that my curiosity suddenly surged. By the age of 13 I was significantly attracted to girls, and found underwear advertisements on the internet more than interesting. My internet searches became increasingly braver. It didn't take long before I was searching for words I would rarely say, urged by conversations I had overheard but not been a part of. I was not one of those kind of guys.

In my inquisitiveness I found more content continually available. Each new click brought a pleasure and an increased desire to discover more of this seemingly harmless, attractive and exciting unknown. The lasso was tightening. I always had self-justification for whatever I searched for. I would let myself think that what I was doing wasn't that bad, after all people were doing much worse. However my conscience would nag at me. I ignored it, as it wasn't very helpful when I was trying to enjoy myself. God was present but I chose to listen to Him only when I wanted to or felt like it. Little did I know this would eventually come swinging back at me. In my internet searching I would avoid words that would associate me with the 'other guys', however soon enough my inquisitiveness and the pull of the lasso was too much, until I eventually typed the four-letter word into a search engine.

The descent

Porn. With that word I plunged deeper into the secret side of my life. I would still justify what I did, not watching the videos I deemed to be 'bad'. I would spend hours searching for something that was the closest reflection of what I felt a normal sexual relationship would look like. I was very picky, choosing carefully what I would click onto and even feeling convicted when I clicked on a video that didn't meet my 'standards'.

By 16 those standards had dropped; I was more insular and the amount of time I would spend searching had greatly increased. Porn had given me a thirst for something I could not meet myself. It was the pleasure that kept me looking, eventually causing me to watch increasingly darker videos. Of course I still justified the secret person that I was becoming. By now I knew the websites and actors by name. I had developed a taste that continually failed to be satisfied.

It was all a ploy and I knew it. I knew because after each session I did not feel satisfied and fulfilled, I didn't feel macho or brave. I felt disgusting. I hated what I was doing. After each session my discomfort was obvious, as God's love for me and my knowledge of the scriptures came rushing in. I felt like I wanted to burn my computer, to cleanse myself of this filth that I felt I was wrapped in. I think up to 80 percent of the time I would pray for forgiveness afterwards. I was always weaning myself off porn, always believing that I was taking steps to become fully detoxed. I deeply regretted ever looking at this material, so I watched videos and read blogs on how to achieve freedom.

It was now incredibly clear to me that I would never find a natural representation of sex in Christian marriage through viewing porn. Nevertheless I would still attempt to find a way to justify my actions. I was hooked and tortured by my inability to escape. To give my mind some rest I even searched for 'Christian porn'. Troubling as that may sound now it shows that my heart was heavy under the balance of knowing what God wanted and struggling with a problem that I just couldn't seem to shake.

By now each session would result in joyless disgust. I was night after night, day after day, literally washing my hands in commitment to never do it again. There was only short-lived physical and emotional relief. I would briefly succeed in conquering the problem for a day or so – a week was an incredible victory. I was in a fluctuating, sporadic battle against my flesh, mind and soul.

Each day I would give in to either just viewing or the accompanying behaviour. Usually one accompanied the other. There were days when I would be consumed, not able to concentrate fully on work or chores. The problem that started so secretly had now become who I was and what I thought about myself. I had become a mask of my original design. I knew what others thought and expected of me but I was so, so far away from that. I continued to be commended for being such a good example. I was trapped in the reputation I had created in my attempt to not be labelled like everyone else. I hated stereotypes so to know I was secretly reinforcing a negative one was crippling. I knew God was still there; I also knew there was a way out – I just couldn't see it.

Failed and trapped

This unsightly darkness was growing inside of me, but, like any secret, I could only hide it for so long. I was constantly trying to cover up when the balancing act just got too much. I particularly struggled in sixth form as I balanced work with my emotional and spiritual baggage. I saw no way out of my issues. My work suffered until eventually I decided to drop out of sixth form, seeing my time there a waste as my grades fell and purpose in life dwindled. As the darkness increased my strength decreased. Any confidence I had that I could beat it was close to none.

I struggled to knock on doors, make phonecalls and look for jobs. I didn't want people to know me. What was I good for, what could I bring? I couldn't dance at parties or draw attention to myself. I tried to hide away who I was. So I quietly covered my shame, maintaining what reputation I had before the darkness hit me again.

I desperately wanted someone strong in the faith to ask me outright what I was struggling with. I wanted someone to initiate the discussion of the problem...but it never came. I couldn't face reaching out to someone because no one ever talked about the issues I faced. It was barely mentioned. It was not a part of Christian conversation. Each time we split down into genders as a youth group I waited for the words to surface, for someone to say 'if you are struggling with the topics mentioned please come and see me after', but they never did. Instead it was just another session on sex that seemed miles away from what my problems were. The truth of how complex and intertwined my problems were was never tackled or even mentioned. This desire to be approached was a constant hope throughout the entirety of the time I struggled, which was almost four years from before I was 16 to almost 20.

I was looking for a way in which I could be reconnected with my purpose and a way in which I could live true to the closeness that others thought I had with God. I needed an escape. I wanted a dramatic conversion, for God to simply take my problem away. The war for who I was continually raged. Because I was now outside of full-time education I had no entry routes to progress and, as I had left at the beginning of the school year, I found myself occupying my time with the two things that fuelled my problems. I did, however, find some solace in discovering a gifting I had with cooking. It gave me a glimmer of hope that I could be useful, good for something. I decided to attend an employability course; it did little to help me with my deep-seated problems but did get me out of the house and focused my mind on other things. As I looked for direction for my life, the abbreviation YWAM would trigger a new season for me.

A new beginning?

Youth With A Mission stood out as something good for me to pursue. I would be in a different country, with different people, doing something that connected me with God and helped other people. I had taken trips away with school, breaks from my caged reality, and they had taught me so much and drew me closer to God. During my trips to India and Romania I really felt I was connected to my purpose and call, and I managed to hold my problem off for the short amount of time I was there. I had freedom, purpose and fun on those trips and that is what I wanted my life to be like. YWAM seemed like it could provide that.

The battle was on, there was a date, a line, a marker in my life when I could start afresh, just like the goal I set myself every birthday, new year and Sunday morning. I managed to fight the dark sessions off for a whole week before I left to go on holiday to Trinidad and then start my Discipleship Training School (DTS) in Barbados. The DTS was the first one that I had looked at on the internet and was justice focused; I felt God had led me to be on it.

My time at YWAM Barbados (July–December 2010) was one of the best times of my life. I confronted my issue and felt I had freedom from it. My identity in Christ was taught and built up. I was reconnected with my original design and to the amazing grace and love of God. I felt the freest I had felt in years. I was doing what I loved, in a part of the world where I was at home, eating food I love and spending time with amazing people. Through one-on-one and open conversations with others, I really rediscovered my passion for justice, which had begun as a boy, and planned to attend the School of Reconciliation and Justice. I began to dream again about how I could help to bring God's love to those who needed it most. I felt that I was on the path that God wanted me to be on. I saw this as the end of my story with porn and its sister, (masturbation of course) – after all it had been six months... However, that story had yet to reach its abrupt ending. Eventually I returned to Bradford.

Bradford was cold. There was no beach, no sea, no one who knew what I had supposedly beaten. There didn't seem to be anyone who shared the same heart as me. It was very different. However, I was grateful for my family and I have fond memories of that Christmastime. As I planned to leave again to attend the School Of Reconciliation and Justice (SORJ) with YWAM Harpenden, I updated two of my closest friends with the fact that I had dealt with the sister problems I had struggled with for many years. It felt good to let people know I was now free and a 'better person' in my own eyes. Christmas came and I received a very generous gift of a laptop to help me in the SORJ that would finish just before my 19th birthday. I was thrilled and soon got used to the independence of having my own computer. I didn't know then that the laptop was to be the trapdoor back to what had plagued my life for so long.

Back to the beginning?

I became unwise with the way I used the internet, spending a long time just entertaining myself. The holiday season and my lack of anything to keep me occupied resulted in my devotional times slipping and my communication with God quietened to a whisper. Honestly? I had simply become lazy. Eventually, as I was browsing the internet I came across a picture that tempted me to look at more, those deceptively 'nice' feelings came again and I ended up having one of my all too familiar sessions in the privacy of my own room. I finished and cried out to God. I had thought this struggle was finished. I spoke to a friend from DTS that had faced similar things, but, after the one mistake quickly multiplied, the embarrassment and obvious distance barrier resulted in conversation drying up to nothing.

The only hope I found in dealing with the issues was in the next line I could draw. I was starting SORJ. So, for the first two months I had no trouble, but, after stumbling accidentally onto a pornographic picture blog, I gave in and covertly indulged in both sides of the battle. I knew that internet usage was monitored on site so I then became paranoid of being kicked out of the Harpenden base. I would rush past the main office building and avoid eye contact and conversation with those I knew were involved with IT management at the base. I lived totally burdened by the lie I was living, and in constant fear of condemnation. I did plan to do the outreach stage of the SORJ but my desperation to be removed from the situation was increasing, and, when I discovered that the outreach would remain on the base, I let the leaders know I would be leaving.

On returning home I was severely ashamed of myself and am still very sorry for breaching the agreement I had when staying at YWAM. I hated the darkness that had come back to bite me twice as hard. I was even tempted to email the base anonymously to let them know of the gap in their online security. I utterly hated what I was doing, but the dreams I had created throughout my time in YWAM were still there. I wanted to equip myself further through the Foundations of Community Development School. I longed to help in places that 'needed me', where I could perhaps shake my problems as I had done in Barbados. I started working at a coffee shop to raise money for the course. But my parents had become disillusioned with my full-time missions. I struggled to re-adapt to the normal world. I couldn't cope with the pressures of my job in combination with my problems and resigned in the hope of finding a job that would be better paid.

From the moment I arrived back in Bradford the battle had intensified, and the fluctuation of times of victory and times of defeat became more extreme. By now I was desperate to shake free of this problem. I wanted to do great things for God but could not build anything on the wounded person I was. The content I viewed had worsened and the time I spent watching increased. I found my only peace within video games that would distract my mind and take me away from the reality I was in. The dreams of another season with YWAM evaporated. There was no way I could get enough money together and my parents couldn't and wouldn't support me, if after six months I would come out the same way I went in. I was stuck at home and began to think of other options for my life. I tried various doors but they closed one after the other. The dreams that I had dwindled as the expectations of my life were continually lowered with each session of defeat and with each closed door. I was nothing, simply wrapped in sin and shame. I could not improve on my life. Things could only get worse.

Never ending story?

I looked back on my time in Barbados as heaven. There I had been free and fulfilled. How could my life get any better than it was then? When I wasn't looking at porn I was looking at places in the world where I could possibly replicate what I had had with the DTS. Soon my thinking became darker and darker. I was convinced that the freedom I longed for I could only find somewhere else, like Barbados. However simply moving away was unlikely to provide the important friendships I had enjoyed two years previously. I found a website where you could volunteer and in exchange receive free housing and food. I began to look for the best place to go to find a last chance of freedom.

With each failure of restraint, my mind was far from looking for forgiveness and instead looked for the best place to escape to. I now was not only battling pornography and its sister but also their cousins; depression and suicide. I never did get enough money to go away, so decided my plans for escape would have to take place closer to home. I remember when I started to write out a goodbye letter, I realised I was wearing a shirt that supported a suicide prevention charity. It just showed how split my life was, but the realisation caused me to stop. I was still Nathan the great Christian guy, who contributed well to homegroup and wanted to change the world, but I now believed I never could. I wished there was a way to die and make it look like an accident. I started to pray that God would take my life.

Then, out of the blue, I received a message on Facebook from someone who did not know me, connected to a forum I had posted on. This was in October of 2011. He wanted to know more about me. 'You sound interesting – what church are you a part of in Bradford?' After I replied for the first time his response contained these words: 'Nathan I sense strongly the hand of God is on your life – very powerfully– that is why you can't escape even though you have drifted and tried. You feel special because you are – that is the favour of God – if He can put that on a sex addict and murderer – King David – He can with you!!'

My response to the message, again showed how completely separate the two parts of my life were. Initially I failed to make the connection between the message and my situation. Yet of all the people the message sender could have likened my life to (Abraham, Moses, Joseph, Elijah, Peter or Paul) he likened me not simply to David, but sex addict David! And David is even my middle name! He also had no way of knowing that I too was thinking of taking a life (just like David) – my own! On top of which I had been plan-ning the 'escape' for months.

After googling the message sender's name I realised this guy had really influenced Christianity. So I wondered why he would even bother contacting me. 'Great!' I thought. 'Yet another person believing I am a wonderful man of God!' I didn't fully understand why he would send a message to me but, looking back, I am amazed I struggled to see its relevance. It was unbelievably relevant! Little did I know that this was the start of a conversation that would go deep inside my heart and really change my whole life.

Another prophecy!

A few weeks later in homegroup, I felt a pressure from the inside of my chest, a strange feeling that urged me to open my mouth. I knew I had to speak in tongues. I interrupted the meeting and explained that I felt like I needed to speak. I spoke in tongues aloud to the group. Eventually as I finished, shaking and full of emotion, two people interpreted what I had said, both confirming each other's understanding. The interpretation was something like this: 'God has not forgotten about you, He has not forgotten your passions and heart and He wants you to draw closer to Him. He has a plan for your life. He loves you.'

I wept and wept at the severe relevance to my situation. God continually showed that He was very real and active and had not forgotten about me. I was still in a stage of darkness, with only one door left to try: to pursue what God had put on my heart. My parents apologised randomly one day in the car for their negativity towards those in full-time ministry. They released me to do whatever I wanted to with God. I was slowly realising that I had to do something. Two of my school friends were involved in ministry but they both worked alongside a pastor in their church. My church didn't have a main pastor and the practicality of how to enter into ministry was foreign to me. I just knew that it was the only option I had left, regardless of my issues. I was already serving in church, so I increased the hours and took on volunteering overnight to help serve the homeless in our area.

During one of these overnight stays on 12 January 2012 I thought I would use the time to call a friend, Ashlee, who lived in Australia. She was one of the friends who knew I had apparently dealt with my issues on my return from DTS. She had always been there to talk, to process and to learn from. I had not spoken to her for six months at this time. I skyped her and our conversation was very different to the usual chat. We were more honest and open than ever before. There was a heightened sense of the warmth I had always felt for her and, as a result of the conversation, we expressed a mutual affection. So, among other things, I told her about the Facebook message and the messenger. She then highlighted the importance of this connection and the fact that this could be the chance I had been looking for, to live out my desire to be in ministry.

In that chair storage room at 3:30am the Holy Spirit turned up. I was shaking and speechless. I felt so loved, chosen and called for who I was and not what I had done. I committed in that moment to remove the obstacles that were before me and run into what God had for me. I knew I had to pursue the connection with the message sender.

In hot pursuit

So the next day I spoke to the man who had sent me the message. He said it was interesting that I contacted him as God had put me on his heart the day before. I told him that I really wanted to be in ministry but I had no pastor to go to. He invited me to go south and visit him. Was there was a possibility there may be something I could be a part of I wondered? After my first visit he invited me again, this time for a leaders' conference. On the first evening he said he would like to ask me a few questions. We sat in the hotel bar and he said to me, 'If you came to join me, is there anything in your past that may pop up that we may have to deal with, or anything that would compromise my ministry? I want to know who I am taking on pastorally.'

For the last few years of my life, I had prayed and waited for someone to ask me that question! Now, at long last, having realised that the other Nathan had no right to exist, and feeling I had started to find my true identity, the question confronted me. I felt I was not simply on the path of freedom from a problem but gathering momentum, progression and transformation into the truth of who God had made me, even though it was only six weeks since 12 January. So why on earth was I being asked this question now?

I realised that I was still highly embarrassed by the issues of my past, but managed to splutter out my story, which I had told no one else about. I did it partly because I wanted to get some integrity and time behind me so I had some experience to stand on. We finished our drinks and went back to our separate rooms. Now, for the first time, I had someone to stay accountable to, someone who knew about my past but didn't harshly judge me. He wanted me to be a part of his life and ministry. This was the Nathan that I really was. This is the Nathan I will always be. The 'gift of God', which is exactly what my name means.

Within weeks my parents and I packed the car and I moved to Leatherhead, Surrey. This was the last place Wesley ever preached but it has been an uphill struggle for any evangelical church to survive here. I am currently at the centre of the leadership team of Pioneer Engage Church. In what seemed like no time at all I was invited to work with a flourishing, high-quality youth ministry, growing in numbers and influence. We were asked by the Leatherhead Festivities Committee to fill every Saturday in December with carols, nativity, Christmas music and dance. Relationships have been steadily growing and we have already seen much fruit from investing in people's lives. We have recently seen a whole bunch of teenagers come to Christ. The basis for all of this is to see a church shaped by the Great Commandment – to love – and the Great Commission – to go.

In case you haven't guessed, the name of the messenger was Gerald Coates. I have been utterly and completely free of my addictions and behaviour since 12 January 2012, praise God! Almost unbelievable!

'The moment sex ceases to be a servant it becomes a tyrant.'

Saint Francis by GK Chesterton

Chapter 2

The First Big Issue –
M or is it a W?

Nathan: To Gerald, M – or masturbation – is a word (some regard as the polite word) that he freely admits he finds 'clumsy and embarrassing'. The reason I use W – as in 'having a wank' – is because that is what my peers use – especially those who are not yet Christians. (Gerald used the word in his introduction but, knowing him as I do, it was probably for shock value!) A friend of Gerald's, Caleb (who wrote in the introduction) was at university and shared a house with five others. He describes how it was not unusual for one of them to say, 'Right guys, studies are over, I am going upstairs to have a wank, so leave me alone for an hour!' Decoded that meant he did not want anyone coming into his room as he would be watching internet porn with his jeans and boxers down – I don't need to describe the rest! When he came downstairs another guy might even ask him how it went! Yes, we polite, decent, sensitive and understandably, somewhat conservative, Christians (who often have a tendency to mainly relate to other Christians) have perhaps been overprotected.

Gerald: As Nathan has explained in his introduction and chapter 1, at the age of 13 the mild sexual urges he felt led to him pleasuring himself. But this developed and became a way of life. Then it became an addiction and he needed more stimuli than his mind could offer. So he partnered with porn. Eventually he was planning most of his Saturdays 'home alone' around the computer.

William, who you will meet towards the end of the book, was even younger when friends talked about wanking and how to do it. Not wanting to be left out, or feeling abnormal, he practised until it became normal. But by the age of 14 he was conjuring up images and by 15 a 17-year-old friend showed him pornographic images – he was horrified! But he had seen the images... It was like dropping a tennis ball into a pile of soot and then throwing it at a white wall – it left its mark.

William had three close friends of a similar age and all were sexually active with girls. His increasing inquisitiveness caused him to access porn himself, 'To see what everyone was up to and what I might be missing'. Like most young men of his age, he felt inadequate and perhaps annoyed that his friends knew more about this stuff than he did.

The progression is similar to addictive drug taking. Soft drugs, used on occasion, need not lead to taking hard drugs. But almost every hard drug user began with soft drugs. There is an obvious causal link and so it is with masturbation and internet porn. If you wanked last night you are more likely to tonight, if you used porn as well, you are likely to use it tonight (or tomorrow night) as well. Some feel their copy book has been seriously blotted. So once a night or three times a day, what does it matter?

Well it matters a lot – as we shall see.

The Bible and solo sex

You probably know that Jewish and Christian scriptures never refer to the M or W words. It is true that Onan 'spilled his semen on the ground' (Genesis 38:9) but this is not a reference to masturbation as the story and context confirms. However, every other form of damaging, promise breaking, God-dishonouring sexual activity is covered throughout scripture. But not a single specific reference to M or W. Quite an omission don't you think?

Or is it? Let's go back to Bible times. The Bible covers several millennia, during which there was no radios to entertain, which today are often full of music with suggestive lyrics. There were no television channels complete with racy, saucy and plainly pornographic images – and certainly no TV channels dedicated to porn, where paid prostitutes perform for the pleasure of others! Films and cinemas complete with X- and R-rated offerings never existed. There were no DVDs to watch in the privacy of your own home. Computers and the millions of pornographic images available for every taste, perversion and practice were not even imagined! No suggestive advertising, billboards, ads in publications or local newspaper offers of outright sex in your own home.

Pornographic magazines in shops never existed, no chat lines, no lewd sex texting offering the quick fix of a W and orgasm. No gay sex in the woods (authorities have cleared two sites in our area of late, after numerous complaints of this occurring) and probably little sexual foul language whereas today, even in the middle-class village I live in, children can be regularly heard using the crudest words in the high street and often on our own road.

It was quite a different world, eh? Oh yes, and there were no skirts the length of wide belts, no see-through blouses, no jeans revealing the colour of the owner's underwear with brand logos. Victoria's Secret and other clothes catalogues featuring men and women in underwear, bikinis or tight-fitting, revealing clothes didn't exist. No – the world of the Middle East was generally very hot, and people wore appropriate loose-fitting clothes, covering neck to toe!

Most people were married during their early teens, whereas marriage at present, for most, takes place 10 to 20 years after sexual awareness occurs. Commentators, theologians and historians are agreed that the Virgin Mary was unlikely to have been much older than 15 years when she married Joseph, who was probably no older than 17 years himself.

So the following words are tough in the sexual culture of the 21st century: 'Don't go to bed with another's spouse', Jesus says, adding, 'But don't think you've preserved your virtue simply by staying out of bed. Your *heart* can be corrupted by lust even quicker than your *body*. Those leering looks you think nobody notices – they also corrupt.' (Matthew 5:27–28, The Message)

Back to the future

Ben (who you will also meet at the end of the book) was only 14 years when it became clear to him that guys at his boys' school were wanking. He discovered it was a commonplace activity, and they made it into a bit of a joke. So he did the same, simply bowing to peer pressure. That led to internet porn and later pressure on relationships.

There was no such sexualised culture within the Jewish community 2,000 years ago, never mind before that (although there was plenty of sex on offer in other places and cultures). By the time Paul came along, 'Rome was full of prostitutes, tax collectors and recorders counted more than 70 brothels merely in the vicinity of the Coliseum!' This sexual freedom, according to historian David Instone-Brewer, 'Was considered scandalous in the Jewish and the Christian world.'[1] And whereas Christ and Peter primarily addressed issues for Jews and later to the born-again Jewish communities, Paul had a different mission audience – mainly non-Jews or Gentiles. He was travelling to places where Christ had not been preached. The Gentile's culture and behaviour was not yet shaped by scripture or the gospel. Rome was not in Israel 2,000 years ago – and remains in Italy to this day! Paul had to address issues that were so different to those Christ or Peter addressed.

For all of us wanting to feel normal, keeping up with the W crowd, Paul's warning to his disciple Timothy is important. Timothy would have joined Paul on his mission trips to decadent Rome and liberalised Greek culture. Timothy no doubt found himself perhaps regularly stirred by 'what came naturally'. This would have been a shock. His eyes instructed the brain, which activated the hormones – now what?

'Flee also youthful lusts; but pursue righteousness, faith, love, peace with those who call on the Lord out of a pure heart.' (2 Timothy 2:22, NKJV) Paul is making things clear;

don't stop to pray, fight or philosophise – no, FLEEEEEEE! By the time appetites have been quietly promised fulfilment in the shower, bed, alone in the house with the laptop or with the girlfriend – it's often too late! You should have fled! That is, run away, divert your gaze, do something else, give someone a call – pray together – don't entertain – don't think about it – RUUUUUN! Don't promise sexual appetites a thing. It will lead to images of old girlfriends, or guys, people you know, or internet porn, being accessed so easily by a very powerful long-term sexual memory.

The mind is either being renewed, cleansed and refreshed, (usually by scripture, Christian books, sung worship and Christian friends) or it is at war with God's pure, clean Spirit! At war your mind will be defensive – resistant – disrespectful – fighting God off.

What's good for the goose!

Life expectancy 2,000 years ago was much lower than it is today. Poverty, sickness, disease, military oppression and war left many young widows. So Paul, having given instructions to young, single men like Timothy, turns his attention to young women – widows: 'The widow who is really in need and left all alone puts her hope in God, and continues night and day to pray and ask God for help. But the widow who lives for pleasure is dead even while she lives.' (1 Timothy 5:5,6)

Sexual gratification with self or with others is all the same to Paul. His question is: is the widow living for God or for pleasure? Single or married, we should all ask the same of ourselves. So – are you living for yourself? That is, are you living for personal pleasure, sexual or otherwise, or are you living a life of regular self-denial – from pleasure days, events and moments – because you have a higher calling; to serve Christ and what He requires of you? Yes I know that CS Lewis wrote that pleasure is God's invention, not the devil's.[2] But there is a difference between enjoying pleasurable views, colours, shapes, textures and smells, friends and private times – than living for them as an end in themselves, at the expense of sacrifice, loyalty and commitment.

Paul was not being principled without pastoral understanding and care. Yes he was once young, single and shaped by scripture – as a well taught Jew. Later he would have been married. He was a member of the Sanhedrin, the highest tribunal of the Jews that met in Jerusalem. There were similar courts in Greece and Rome. But you had to be married to be a member. As Paul never mentions his wife it is assumed she probably died or even left him. Then he became opposed to the Living God and His people. But, following his dramatic conversion, he lived out his ministry as a single person and because of the persecution, and sometimes martyrdom, suffered by the first believers, suggested it was better to be single than married with a wife and children. Certainly he travelled and taught in ways that would have been almost impossible if married. Such sacrifice is rare in modern evangelicalism with its focus on the family and faint suggestion that something might be 'wrong' if a guy is in his 40s and single. Shame – a great shame!

In fact at one stage Paul gives the only reason the New Testament provides for marriage. It's basic to say the least! 'Now to the unmarried and the widows I say: It is good for them to stay unmarried, as I do. But if they cannot control themselves, they should marry, for it is better to marry than to burn with passion. The difficulties of marriage are preferable by far to a sexually tortured life as a single.' (1 Corinthians 7:8–9, The Message)

So – no M or W? An impossible dream?

Nathan: Yes I am back – and importantly, as far as Gerald is concerned, I am around the age of many of our readers.

In the light of scripture and experience, I have reached a conclusion. It took me quite a while to come to this conclusion; it has followed four years of frequent and at times daily use of pornography and the behaviour that goes with it. Sure, I would have been relatively happy if there was less frequency and activity. But I was looking for far more than simply a lessening of my addiction. It seemed I had an impractical dream of being completely free. Now looking back over a year I realise the impossible dream (no M or W) is the only possible way to live fully for Christ. Maybe there will be occasional failings, (but not so far!), I am just being realistic. So the issue is how did I get away from the continual pull of a contaminated thought life to where I am now – happy and free?

What were the factors that came into my life to change my thinking? What were the changes and how did they affect me?

Well, to start with, I had to ask, 'what do I want?'

To begin to understand *how* I got free, you have to understand *why* I wanted to be free. You are not reading this book because you are perfectly comfortable with your behaviour; you are reading it because you want to conquer the problems that you are facing, or gain momentum and strength in your effort to overcome. We need to know where we are now so we can live the opposite way. We must begin to identify, remove and replace the behaviour and addiction that has corrupted our stories from their original intention.

The identification of how we feel, why we feel that way and our response to our feelings make up the first step out of our situations. That in mind, what did I feel in my situation and what may you feel in yours? What are the strongholds of our thinking (a stronghold is anything that has a strong hold over us – simple) and how do they cause us to act differently from someone who is free?

My behaviour had stained me and made me feel uncomfortable in my own skin. It corrupted the way I looked at others and at myself. I felt useless, purely because of what I was stained by. I felt unable to do certain things or live in a certain way. I felt unfulfilled, believing that whatever I did well or did 'right' would fall through the chasm of my problems. I felt as if I had no integrity. Anything I would try to achieve, or even succeed at, would be simply comparing a rice grain of purity with a skyscraper of sin. I felt unable to receive affection. Who I was did not deserve reward. I felt separated from the source of all joy, happiness and fulfilment – God. It was as if salvation did not exist to me, even though I called God my Saviour.

Although I was colourful public Christian I was a private scandal.

One of the biggest lies that the devil sows through our failings is that our sin defines who we are. This says that we *can't* be free, we are *not* loved and we *cannot* be used for God's Kingdom. The lie pulls us back to addiction time after time. Once we deal with that lie we can then begin reconstructing lifestyles and thinking mechanisms so that we can walk in the freedom and purity that God has already provided. I can give you all the advice you want about the practical steps to take but if your thinking doesn't change you will have no motivation and strength to walk into freedom.

Repentance is basically a change of thinking that can precede a change of behaviour. In retrospect, before 12 January I knew all along what I needed to do, but because my thinking didn't change, every time I tried I failed – because I felt I was a failure. I felt there was no point even trying to become free because I was already engulfed in sin. It seemed too hard and I had tried too many times before.

Light or darkness?

Once we have identified how we feel, exposing the physical results of our problem, we can see the root. This is the perception that our sin defines who we are, consciously or not. Once we cast light onto the issues we can identify things for what they really are and boldly name them. So now I'm going to name them: pornography, wanking, lust, cover-ups and outright lies. These words and actions must not master us, we must master them. I allowed sexual perversion (because that's what it was) to replace these words with generalities. When we stand back and look at what affect these words have on our lives as people of God, we realise that we are not the problem, our sin is. Our second step of action is to know and live in the truth.

'He is the atoning sacrifice for our sins, and not only for ours but also for the sins of the whole world.' (1 John. 2:2)

Jesus took our sin away when we chose to enter into salvation. What we have done, or will do, cannot affect our eternal worth as we seek to journey closer to Him. The truth is that we are free from sin through Christ, so that we can enter into a relationship with God. 'Moreover, the Father judges no one, but has entrusted all judgement to the Son.' (John 5:22)

It is this truth the Bible says, that sets us free. How are we then set free by this truth?

As Gerald often says, 'God never gets disillusioned with us, He never had any illusions in the first place!'

The truth that I just outlined needs to form the basis of the way we live and the way we see ourselves. If we choose to live upon this truth and rebuke the lies, we can live differently. However truth in itself cannot set us free. Jesus' best friend John explained they had seen the glory of God, 'full of grace and truth'. (John 1:14)

An awareness of God's grace prepares us for the truth. 'The Word became flesh and blood, and moved into the neighbourhood. We saw the glory with our own eyes, the one-of-a-kind glory, like Father, like Son.' (John 1:14, The Message)

Jesus was in my neighbourhood, I grew up with Him. I just never fully opened the door to welcome Him. I rarely listened to Him knocking. So rather than the inseparable friend He should be, He was someone I looked out the window at, admired from a distance but never answered. The very nature of truth means that we must base our lives and our thinking on it. If we don't base our lives and thinking on the fact that Jesus loves us and has set us free from sin then it is not truth to us. If we are not living in it, we can't receive the freedom. The lies of the enemy separate us from the truth that we are precious and loved, that through salvation Jesus has made us so much better than people enslaved by the sister problems.

Nothing 'shall be able to separate us from the love of God.' (Romans 8:39, KJV) We can, however, be separated from the truth of what His love brings and what that means for us as His children.

Message and messengers

For me the message, the messenger, the interpretation, the confession and finally Ashlee filled me with the wonder of God's grace. Each act of grace was an increasingly louder knock at my door, knocks that I could no longer miss – or drown out. This grace caused me to push the doors wide open for Jesus to come in. It allowed me to further under-stand, accept and apply the truth.

Okay. You may not have received a Facebook message, been able to make a confession or have a friend who can be part of the unique displays of grace that I was blessed with. But I never had the book you are holding! We are praying for you, that this book, my story and Gerald's insights will provide the catalyst for breaking strongholds in your life. The amazing way that God brought us together and enabled us to write this book is surely the grace of God for you and any of your friends who are trapped in the behaviour and addictions that I once found myself in.

> 'How can a young person stay on the path of purity? By living according to your word.' (Psalm 119:9)

The direction we want our lives to head in is toward this truth. We need to replace our damaged thinking with the truth. The truth is that we can be reconciled to a loving, fulfilling, restorative relationship with God. The truth is He has paid the price for our sins, we can be free and He is working in and through us. So we reflect upon that truth and apply it to our life. We commit to living according to God and scripture. Our thinking must not be shaped by our condition; it must be shaped by God's words.

Ben John was 16 years old when he found pornography and accessed it several times a week. He slowly realised this viewing and attendant behaviour was the cause of dishonesty and cover-ups. By age 19 he was in serious trouble. Fearing his computer might be monitored he used his iPhone instead. Wanting an encounter with God he went to a large conference Gerald was participating in. Gerald, knowing nothing of his situation, gave him words of prophetic encouragement. After Ben went home he contacted Gerald and discovered that we were writing, but did not know what the book was about. Later Ben explained his situation. It was serious. But the conference encounter, combined with scripture and prophecy, brought the entire mess to an immediate halt. Months later, there has not been one single instance of Ben looking at, or for, porn (you can read more of his story in chapter 9).

Standing in liberty

'Stand fast therefore in the liberty by which Christ has made us free, and do not be entangled again with a yoke of bondage.' (Galatians 5:1, NKJV)

A yoke is a wooden neckpiece that holds a pair of oxen together. It was a common sight in Bible times.

So when we feel tempted to get entangled in damaging sin, we can deflect it with the truth. That is, we don't need to view and misbehave, and we will also find increasingly that we don't want to. In my own journey into freedom I rebuked the lies and the temptation in the name of Jesus. It's when we feel like visiting hell that we must touch heaven. Worship enables us to be in a place of surrender where we can meet with His Spirit, His love. When we learn to surrender the lies, surrender what we think of ourselves and be open to God, He can touch our spirit with His love, and we can be reminded of our true identity in Him and be reminded that we have a choice.

Once we learn how to make this connection and practice it, it strengthens us. We can take what we have learnt in the way we worship, however that may be, and apply it to our day-to-day lives so we can call upon God's presence at any time, not simply in set 'worship sessions'. This creates disciplined rhythms of reflection and meditation on the truth of scripture that that we can continually build our lives upon, and which help us to shape direct channels to His power. We begin to rewrite the negative psychological connections our brain makes, causing a stronger path of thinking to be formed.

So, to summarise: I unwrapped my identity from my actions when I realised that my thinking had been influenced strongly by lies that created thoughts that are untrue and a presumption towards judgement that kept me trapped. I acknowledged the truth of the situation of who I really was in God's eyes and what He had done for me through Christ's life, death and resurrection. Through grace I accepted the truth. Now I live in the recognition that we have a choice in our actions, that His power to overcome is readily available to us. We do not need to engage in the problems that have plagued this generation; we are not weak. He has made us strong.

Notes

1. 'New Testament Scandals', *Christianity* magazine, 2009.
2. CS Lewis, *The Screwtape Letters*, chapter 9.

Chapter 3

The C in the Room, the P in the Pocket

She is easier than love
It's easier than life
It's easier to fake and smile and bribe

It's easier to leave
It's easier to lie
It's harder to face ourselves at night
Feeling alone,
What have we done?
What is the monster we've become?

'Easier than love' by Switchfoot

Nathan: This song may be a few years old, however its relevance is the same now as it was then. I for one have known how much easier it is to lie and hide away problems rather than confronting them. Today's technology makes it easy to erase the history of what we have viewed – we even have the choice not to record it at all. We carry the capability to access a plethora of incredibly helpful or severely detrimental content in a matter of seconds. A tool that we often have to use for school, work or church can become something that could nullify our involvement in those very places. Through mobile internet and Wi-Fi the temptation is quite literally living with us.

Laptops, mobile phones and tablets are typically personal

and often used in the privacy of our own room when we are alone. They are used as tools for our entertainment, assistants for our work and they connect us to the rest of the world. Social networking websites allow us to portray ourselves exactly how we want to be seen. However, along with our likes and our successes, what is *not* shown are our failings and personal struggles. There seems to be little room for humility when there are so many onlookers into our lives.

We should probably add 'the T in the bag' to this chapter's title, to make it: 'The computer in the room, the tablet in the bag and the phone in the pocket'. Each one of these items can act as wonderful facades to mask the corrosive behaviour in our tender lives. In a world where image is said to be everything, we can easily be swayed to behave in a particular way, and to say the right lines on the right cues. It is no wonder that those with behaviour that isn't so marketable are pressured to greatly increase the void between who they are publicly and who they are privately.

Let's face it, we can't avoid being influenced in some way by what we are connected to and are around each day. Let's not, though, call it secondhand smoke if we are puffing away on several a day. We can unintentionally see and be influenced by a behavioural trigger or we can go searching for it. We have a choice of what we are connected to, how much time we spend doing it and how we let it affect our lives (more on this later). If we can't avoid being influenced by what we are around, then we must do is choose what we are around the most.

What a din!

We can spend hours at a time online, filling the gaps between the activity in our lives with noise. Well, not entirely sound; rather the clash of images, games and activity that are shallow and unconstructive. This 'stuffing' can act as a distraction from the reality in which we live, filling the time we could use purposefully with a barrage of what could be seen as a more attractive use of our time. This din we fill our lives with is often what we *want* to hear. They can be attractive sounds that everyone else seems to listen to; the beat that the world marches to. We may become more in sync with the beat of the world than with the beat of God's advancing Kingdom and the moments of silence when God speaks.

> Then he [Elijah] was told, 'Go, stand on the mountain at attention before GOD. GOD will pass by.' A hurricane wind ripped through the mountains and shattered the rocks before GOD, but GOD wasn't to be found in the wind; after the wind an earthquake, but GOD wasn't in the earthquake; and after the earthquake fire, but GOD wasn't in the fire; and after the fire a gentle and quiet whisper. (1 Kings 19:12, The Message)

The Bible is full of din, not all of it bad, but God is looking for us to take time away from the noise to reflect and to hear His voice. Often the noise of the world causes us to lose any restraint over our thinking, which means that we no longer make purposeful choices but are caught up in following our wants and our culture rather than our needs.

We all live fast-paced lives; it's no different for us here in Leatherhead. Recently, the leaders and trustees decided to fast in expectancy for an exciting season in the life of Pioneer Engage Church. Julie, a very intelligent woman on our board of trustees, decided to fast from television soaps. On reflection she realised what 'complete and utter rubbish' she was watching, filling her eyes and ears with a false reality that altered the way she perceived the world and others. Soap operas were Julie's din. Julie found several more hours a week where she could reflect, read, feed her soul and listen to God. This came from a replacement of the din in her life with the quiet of reflection. What is your din? What can you replace it with?

Joshua George's din was the unhappiness of his early years. This led him to abuse himself, then to comfort himself through the pleasure of wanking. But the pain and the pleasure combined to create an addiction that not a soul knew about. But God knew and came to his case. (Another man you'll meet in chapter 9!)

Hold on, isn't connectivity a good thing? It is! It's a great thing. Let's not throw the baby out with the bathwater. Banning computers from homes and the use of the internet has been done in Christian households before. The holy axe fell on what has been deemed to be 'of the world'. I don't however take that view, which I guess is obvious as I am typing on a computer connected to the internet with my smartphone to the left of me. Here is the point where a God of resurrection and renewal comes into play. This is the God who works everything together for the good of those who love Him (Romans 8:28). So He can use the internet – and He has! I may not be typing this now if it hadn't been for the two displays of grace that were shown to me through the internet. We can access teaching, praise, international missions, micro-financing schemes, conference streaming, child sponsorship, entertainment, interest networks, games, recipes and can even get to speak with a beautiful friend from across the pond. The internet is great if used with purpose and diligence. Again, it goes back to obedience of the scriptures to do everything for the glory of God: 'Therefore, whether you eat or drink, or whatever you do, do all to the glory of God'. (1 Corinthians 10:31, NKJV)

Stepping back from our online behaviour and disposition, what else wouldn't we be too happy to do in front of God? What things are not pleasing to Him? What behaviour causes you to eventually end up watching porn? Gerald often says: 'If it's not happening in heaven it shouldn't be happening on earth.' Or would you rather there was porn in heaven?

I want to target the very behavioural sequence that takes place before viewing porn. I am discussing what other websites, what other searches could potentially lead us to view things that are not helpful. My intention in doing this is not to blacklist trigger websites. My intention is that through the following questions you can transform the outcome of time spent online. So: how are you spending your time online? Why do you search for the things you do? Is that helpful for your journey? When we are online we must make that time sacred, connected to God.

'When nothing is sacred, there's nothing to lose
When nothing is sacred, all is consumed.'
'Selling the news' by Switchfoot

Time but none online

I mentioned earlier that it's easy to fill the space in our lives with the noise of internet activity. That time doesn't need to be useless, wasteful and unconstructive. What if we could use the 31 hours plus we spend online each week[1] to glorify God through the sites we visit, content we talk about and the things we watch? It starts with being intentional with the time we spend. We mustn't simply open up our browser to be swept away with what we fancy doing at the time, but stop even before we do that to ask: what do I want to do online today? Is it helpful? Do I need to do it? How long do I need to spend doing it? By asking these questions we can do more of the beneficial things we want to do in less time.

We shouldn't forget what a deceptive, corrupting world lies just a few taps away. As I have already said, I would tap to the very fringe of what I deemed acceptable, which is how I came to search for Christian porn. We flirt with what isn't labelled. Poison doesn't need to have a label to be harmful. We can fool ourselves all too easily by walking along the fence of porn, a low fence that can easily be jumped. However, if we were intentional with the time we have, there would be no reason for us to wander to a place we must not be.

My unexpected day of deliverance, the 12 January, saw my hours on the computer drop significantly as I realised that I had a choice about how to use my time. I was now aiming for a life that was defined by specific targets – entirely oppo-site to the destructive one I had before. It's amazing how much your life changes when you ask those three questions:

how are you spending your time online? Why do you search for the things you do? Is that helpful for your journey? I asked those questions over and over, until I had built a new structure around how I could welcome God into my entertainment, not simply entertain my flesh. Here I am today, and I can look back and pinpoint times when I became slack with those questions. This occasional sloppiness resulted in me realising there is indeed a direct correlation between the time I spend entertaining myself and the number of times I am tempted. Thank God the three questions can create a firewall that hinders me from returning to the same behaviour that nearly ruined my life and my calling.

This chapter is challenging for me, as it is causing me to analyse my own life now. I am reminded of how I started out. I am forming new, powerful habits that leave no room for old ones. When these new habits form the way we think, they will start to shape the way we act. 'I need downtime though, I need to relax!' I can hear your cries through the words I type, as I myself voiced that complaint. After further scrutiny of my time I realised that I had become so used to the computer, games console or television being the only ways I could unwind that I forgot what I enjoyed doing and wanted to be seen doing. Don't believe the lie that you *need* a screen to unwind. Be intentional with your relaxation, break the complacency that you may find yourself in and do something else! Please don't tell me there is nothing to do, be creative. Feed your mind, get outside. Make yourself into the kind of person that you aspire to be.

To give you an example, after picking up a book by Tom Wright (thanks Oscar!), I found myself incredibly informed, entertained and my soul edified. I had forgotten how much I enjoyed reading. Meanwhile my computer was asleep...

Blind and maimed

Let's not pretend that this is easier than it really is. If you want to live a morally pure life, here's what you have to do: you have to blind your right eye the moment you catch it in a lustful leer. You have to choose to live one-eyed or else be dumped on a moral trash pile. And you have to chop off your right hand the moment you notice it raised threateningly. Better a bloody stump than your entire body being discarded for good in the dump. (Matthew 5:29–30, The Message)

Trying to turn pages with one hand is difficult, made more so if you only have the use of one eye. Does this passage speak against all of us who have lusted, lashed out or both? I am typing with both my hands viewing with both my eyes. Should I repent of disobedience? I don't think I have seen even the most literalist Christian with a hook and an eye patch. I don't think God wants us to end up all looking like pirates! I would hope to think He was simplifying that idea into an engaging and amusing way to remember what to do in the situation He raised.

Jesus spoke drastically because such sin requires drastic action. Blind eyes can't lust just as someone without hands can't raise them in violence. However, blind eyes can still imagine and maimed people can still hurt others. Jesus knew this, which leads me to conclude that He wasn't talking literally. That said, are we doing everything we can short of blinding and maiming ourselves? Our thinking controls our eyes and hands, so to really stop we must not simply cut our activity but remove the thinking that causes us to act in the first place.

So how do we metaphorically blind our eyes and cut off our hands? From the 12 January I did this by asking the question: do I need to go online? It continually led me to answer, 'No, I really don't'. This may be a good start for some of you on your journey to fast from the things that you use to access porn. Taking the computer out of your room is a good start to challenging the way you think about why you use it. I suggest putting it in a place away from where you spend most of your time. For those who have to keep it in your room, how about completely switching it off from the power? This creates a barrier so that you have a chance to think before you log on. Deliberately creating time for you to remember who you are and what you stand for is vital. The more you do this the less you will find you need the computer. So when you do eventually stop your laptop fast, your thinking and right questioning remain.

Internet filters may be the next step to take, so that, if you do find yourself searching or typing in words that you know are not going to be helpful, you are prevented from going any further. There are several available that either outrightly block or send your history to an accountability partner.[2] It may not always be porn that you need to block. If you have a particular friend on a social networking site that posts pictures of themselves that you know aren't helpful for you to look at, opt out of seeing their posts. Really, if you know the triggers, you can stay away from them. Fasts and filters are great steps *towards* stopping, not solutions to, porn addiction. We can stop ourselves accessing porn, however we don't simply want to stop accessing it, we want to stop our cravings and urges to see it.

The filter of our minds is much stronger than the filter on our computer.

A holy hatred

I know from personal experience that we can find ways of removing any barriers in our way if we really want to. The key for us is not to be simply stopped by the filter but to be reminded of the journey we are on and the choice we have. If an internet filter simply serves as a preventive measure, stimulus will be found from elsewhere and our thinking will not change. If it acts as a reminder as well as a barrier it is so much more effective. But barriers alone are not enough in a battle; you need weapons. I have already mentioned connecting with God's Spirit and praying against temptation. One weapon in our arsenal is to ask for holy hatred of porn and its sister. When we ask, God is faithful. It shouldn't surprise us if we do indeed burn with an active hatred of the objectification and corruption of sex in porn.

Gerald and I have both prayed this prayer. I am strongly influenced by God's heart for injustice. What really set a fire against porn in me happened during a Hope for Justice conference. The threats, violence and injustice linked with pornography are very real, even though invisible to voyeurs. The extent of the link between human trafficking and pornography is written about in an article from Covenant Eyes. A few simple searches on this issue can inform you of the massive injustice that lurks beneath the surface.[3]

Our priority should not be to remove the access to negative triggers. Instead our priority should be to transform our thinking and living so that we can be the most effective disciples of Jesus Christ that we can be. We should be changing our lives so that we can spend more time in fellowship with Him. Changing the shape of how we use our time is not enough; we must rethink the very purpose of how our time can be used.

I don't say that flippantly. It is a struggle but it is necessary if we want to live out our freedom and please God with a life that seeks to do His will. I said to myself in the past, 'I'm not perfect though, how can I be expected to live in such a radical way?' The answer to that came in the following verse: 'Be perfect, therefore, as your heavenly Father is perfect'. (Matthew 5:48)

This gem of a one liner comes after Jesus explains that it's simple to act like the rest of the world does; to love those who love you, welcome those that welcome you. Jesus says that to live like the world does gains no reward. We see repeatedly in scripture that living a Christian life is to work toward a perfect (or mature) life. Jesus lived a perfect life, not just a good one. We see transformation in our lives through our decision to be Christ-like. Choosing to live well won't get the same result. So choose to be perfect with how you use your phones, computers and tablets, or, more importantly, be perfect within your thinking and intention of what they can be used for. Don't just settle for 'good'.

'A revolution's not easy when there's civil war on the inside.'

'Breathe' *by Anberlin*

Notes

1. http://www.telegraph.co.uk/technology/4574792/Teenagers-spend-an-average-of-31-hours-online.html *The Telegraph*, Cyber Centennial, 10 February 2009
2. List of accountability/filtering resources suggested by others: X3 watch (www.x3watch.com), Covenant Eyes (www.covenanteyes.com) and Open DNS (Free filtering service) (www.opendns.com)
   For a thorough list see: http://christianity.about.com/od/practicaltools/tp/christianisps.htm
3. http://www.covenanteyes.com

Chapter 4

The + & H

Gerald Coates: This chapter on same-sex attraction could be divided into two parts. The first is the issue of being attracted to another guy and how to respond as a follower of Christ. The second part deals with the wider issues of the so-called 'Gay' scene, media-friendly images and messages as well as health issues, particularly HIV and AIDS. Having sex with just one person, several or many, is never merely personal. Multiplied by millions it affects the very fabric of society.

As Christ's disciples we have to ask: are we simply wanting to create a better church for our friends and families – or a better society?

Well, where do we start? In the current PC, TV-driven climate this may be regarded as the most controversial chapter in the book. And for some it will be the most liberating. What does Christ, the cross and scripture say about this subject and to those directly affected? These are not only important, biblical and moral issues – they often involve painful, sensitive and relational tensions, fears, guilt and sometimes heartbreak. So we need to tread softly but clearly.

If, as we have explained, our sexuality is complex, same-sex attraction is so much more complex.

There are numerous reasons why two people of the same sex having sex is regarded by some as 'less than the ideal'. Others just feel uneasy about the virtual or actual redesign of marriage across a nation. These perspectives are important – many people hold such views, within and beyond the Christian community. These people do not hate homosexuals – they are not bigots. In my experience it is often Christians, or the spiritual, who give up careers and lucrative employment to give unconditional care to homosexuals who have acquired HIV or AIDS. We accept biblical values and behaviour around the themes of loyalty, generosity, honesty, integrity, the protection of the vulnerable, commitment, agreeing agreeably, fidelity – faithfulness and the right to express an informed opinion. And this is particularly true of this subject.

'I disagree with what you say, but I will defend to death your right to say it' is attributed to Voltaire the French Philosopher.[1] But when it comes to this issue, there are a few who do want to silence all views other than their own. I was on a radio show recently and this subject came up – I gave a reasoned, sensitive response. Another panellist blurted out, 'You have no right to come on this programme with these views...' and then realised what he was saying. His unfinished words tailed off into muted embarrassment. If people have no right to a reasoned, experienced and informed view then we are in trouble! Should any group have the right to remove the rights and voices of another? This isn't tolerance or liberalism but fundamentalism!

In 2012, for example, it was reported in the national press that Scottish police forces have been advised not to accept free Bibles as scripture condemns homosexuality.[2] So this issue is certainly complicated and controversial.

Why? Well, when it comes to same-sex attraction or activity, we have to deal with a wide range of issues. These include romantic love, Section 28, human rights, pastoral care, our DNA, tolerance, sexual identification, HIV/AIDS, political correctness, procreation and original intention.

It is questionable whether just one of these issues proves a conclusive case for the rightness or wrongness of same-sex activity. But together? Let's discover!

Original intention

Some people accept the biblical creation story of six days as literal. Many other committed evangelical Christians do not.

However we are not writing about the finer points of scriptural interpretation in this particular book. Suffice to say that evangelicalism understood the language of Genesis 1–3 to be the same as the book of Revelation. It was pictorial, metaphorical, based on imagery – but was telling a truthful story.

Then less than 100 years ago there was a resurgence of a form of the rational based scholasticism movement that was to develop into liberal modernism, putting evangelicalism on the back foot. Today most liberal churches are in serious decline, while the majority of evangelical churches have experienced considerable growth. Why?

Within evangelicalism there are varying points of view, but all tend to place a high value on scripture as well as pastoral care. Traditions can be important, but are less of an issue and such churches tend to be a lot more flexible.

However – in the literal or illustrative story of Adam and Eve, God approved of His creation and told them: 'Be fruitful and increase in number and fill the water in the seas, and let the birds increase on the earth'. (Genesis 1:22)

For thousands of years, this was the norm. It involved a man and a woman, the man's human sperm and the woman's human egg. Were it not so, none of us would be here today.

There is no scriptural evidence that any other model, including men in relationship, having sex with men (or women with women) is either approved of or encouraged in the Old or New Testament. If it is not the norm it is not normal. So this provides us with some pastoral complexities.

In an excellent article, senior research fellow and biblical scholar David Instone-Brewer wrote, 'I am a non-practicing adulterer!' He is stating the obvious of course. All married men or those in committed relationships will find themselves attracted to other women. But what, he asks, 'if I said "I'm a non-practicing homosexual"'?[3]

It is clear the Bible disapproves of same-sex practice.

'Do not have sexual relations with a man as one does with a woman; that is detestable.' (Leviticus 18:22)

'For this reason God gave them up to vile passions. For even their women exchanged the natural use for what is against nature. Likewise also the men, leaving the natural use of the woman, burned in their lust for one another, men with men committing what is shameful, and receiving in themselves the penalty of their error which was due.' (Romans 1:26–27)

'The law is not made for a righteous person, but for the lawless and insubordinate, for the ungodly and for the sinners, for the unholy and profane, for murderers of fathers and murderers of mothers, for manslayers, for fornicators, for sodomites, for kidnappers, for liars, for perjurers...' (1 Timothy 1:9–10)

It is interesting that these issues are nearly always addressed in the context of heterosexual *wrongdoing*. The writers are not just focusing on homosexuals. Scripture does not condemn opposite sex, same-sex or both sex *attraction*. Yet God's position, made clear in the scriptures, was counter-cultural. This was true before, during and following the birth, death and resurrection of Christ. The Roman culture, for example, allowed same-sex activity providing there was no rape. However for a Roman to play the passive role was disdained, it was regarded as weak and effeminate. So Romans were allowed to use slaves instead. Lesbianism (women having sex with women) is never mentioned in Greek or Roman literature. Brewer points out that the only recorded case is of a poetess, Sappho, who lived around 600BC on the Greek Island of Lesbos, which is where we get the word lesbianism from. But the notions of her sexuality were not realised until the 19th century.

So the normal, general and acceptable view of opposite sex relationships and offspring is clear.

Even in the 21st century, we still do not know the reasons for same-sex attraction. Bad parenting, a distant father, a male friend teaching another about masturbation or even childhood sex abuse – all of these could be factors in convincing a guy he is gay. However, in doing research for this book, we were somewhat surprised at the number of guys we talked to who were taught how to masturbate by an older brother or friend, yet none of them as far as we know became involved in homosexual relationships. In fact we know plenty of guys who fit some of these categories, who have a girlfriend or are happily married with children.

On the other hand, we know of one guy who was attracted to a young woman. They courted, were married and had a beautiful baby girl. A few years later he decided he was gay and left her for his boyfriend with whom he had been having sexual relations for some years. However it seems that this change of orientation only works one way.

It's complex guys!

As we have said, and will say many times more, these issues are complex. Daniel was in his mid-teens when, on a hot sunny day, he went for a long walk with a trusted male friend. Eventually they sat down for a rest and then lay back, enjoying the warmth of the sun and chatting about mundane issues of life. Daniel's friend turned over and in a playful manner ran his fingers up and down Daniel's shirt, eventually landing a little lower. Daniel was somewhat taken aback, but, because this was his friend and they were having fun, he felt safe, so he did the same to his friend. This was, he thought, just a pleasant and playful moment in their friendship. Many weeks later the two of them were in John's bedroom, playing computer games. After a while his friend said, 'do you remember what happened when we went for that walk?' Dan, still feeling safe, replied 'of course'. 'Well shall we do it again, but this time with all of our clothes off?' It all seemed silly, but Daniel still felt safe and secure. Sufficient to say they undressed and had sex. There was no kissing, affection or romantic feelings, just magnetic lust and excitement. It was referred to again, weeks later with a further invitation. But Dan was concerned his mother would find out and declined. Then one Sunday at a Christian meeting, people were invited forward for prayer. Dan responded, and burst into tears. He confessed he didn't want to be gay, had experienced sex with his male friend, but wanted to be married and have a family. But he now eroticised about guys his age. He ended up on my doorstep and told his story. I listened carefully and concluded, 'You are not gay, you will get married and have a family'. The young adult was shocked. I further explained that sex on your own or with someone else, providing it is not forced, is meant to be pleasurable. It's the only way our species continue to exist. Then I explained that because he was pleasured by this experience, it did not mean he was 'gay' or destined to a life of same-sex relationships. His pastor 'phoned a while later and said, 'We don't know what you said, but he is completely different, laughing, joking and enjoying friends and life'.

If there is no evidence at present that same-sex attraction is in our DNA then it is a choice, albeit motivated by genuine feelings. We shall look at that a little later...

In conclusion the original intention seems clear. The norm was, and remains, a man and a woman, in a committed relationship, enjoying intimacy and sex, usually resulting in children. No other model seems approved of anywhere in scripture. But there is more.

DNA

It was in 1953 that Francis Crick and James Watson discovered DNA.

Today genetic factors are largely accepted as being the scientifically proven reason for homosexuality. But, as I have said, there are, as of now, no such scientific conclusions! The 1995 *Journal of Homosexuality* published four issues (Volumes 1–4) on the question of biological causes for same sex attraction. These issues were later re-published under the title *Sex, Cells and Same Sex Desires*, edited by John P. De Cecco and David A Parker.

Their conclusion? 'Current research for a possible biological basis of sexual preference has failed to produce any conclusive evidence.' Since then, no new scientific replicated studies have even claimed to find a biological cause for same sex attraction.

In 1999, following a two-year study, Canadian scientists concluded that there was no basis for the discredited 'gay gene' theory.[4]

Peter Tatchell, the gay rights activist, responded, 'I'm amazed that it's taken so long to destroy what is obviously a totally implausible theory. It is a choice and we should be glad it's that way and celebrate it for ourselves.'[5]

Most researchers accept that homosexuality is a very complex mix, possibly of environment, learned behaviour, maybe genetics and personal choice. But it is amazing that here we are in the 21st century and there is still no conclusive scientific proof!

Oscar Wilde's grandson Merlin Holland repudiates the idea that Wilde was homosexual from his schooldays. Referring to Wilde's correspondence, he writes:

He seems to have been infatuated with Florence Balcombe, (who later married Bram Stoker), for two years until he left Oxford in 1878, and had previously flirted with other young women in Dublin. He married Constance Lloyd in 1884, swiftly had two children with her, and by his own account was blissfully happy in the first few years of his marriage. His conversion to homosexuality probably came about in 1886/7 with a young man whom he was to remain a lifelong friend, Robert Ross.[6]

Therefore, despite Lady Gaga, we have no evidence to believe, we were: 'Born this way'.

That said, several guys we have spoken to have stated that they sensed they were gay before puberty (some as young as three years old). As they were not sexually active, (masturbation/pornography), this is in fact impossible. It was pointed out by one researcher that these cases, far from being homosexual, are homo-emotional! More of that issue later as well...

However it is harmful to pretend or deny same gender

attraction. But it is the eroticisation of same-sex friendships or heroes that leads guys to nurture their feelings, often through gay porn and masturbation, which can later lead to physical involvement.

For a while the mantra of the same-sex propaganda machine (a tiny minority of gay people) was 'it is not our fault – it's genetic'. But the homosexual atheist Matthew Parris has recently written: 'We are not two tribes – the straight and the gay.' He continued that for almost all recorded history, humanity described male same-sex activity as, 'a kind of habit, a diversion to which any man might be prone' and concluded same-sex activity is 'something men do as opposed to something men are'. He concludes that many so-called gay men 'manage the considerable intellectual contortion' of believing there is nothing they can do to change their own sexuality, while at the same time, they believe there is quite a lot they can do to alter the straight sexuality of another straight man they fancy. 'Five pints of lager is the usual prescription', he mused. He continued that he hates the plea 'I can't help it' adding, 'It isn't accepted as an argument for paedophilia and shouldn't be. Why, he asks, cannot a man straight or gay boast that he chose?'[7]

Romantic love

'The very essence of romance is uncertainty' wrote the author, playwright, raconteur and homosexual, Oscar Wilde in his *The Importance of being Ernest*.

Romance and uncertainty? Yes of course – will he like me, will he not? Heart pounding, flirtatious behaviour, eye contact and peals of laughter are normal. As is friendly, affectionate touch. But from counselling and support experience, I have to say that the route from attraction and romance to amorous romance and sex between most guys is a very short one.

When we 'fall in love' we are infatuated. To a degree, we are being deceived. We are in love with a fantasy that probably doesn't exist. We are flattered the other person has taken an interest in us. But there are all sorts of things that we have experienced throughout life, actions we have committed, relationships that have gone wrong and a dark side to our make-up, it might take years to share – if ever. This is not obvious at first glance!

And to encourage two wounded and often confused people together – on the basis of looks, physical attraction, sexual fantasy, personality and sense of humour – is often a recipe for considerable pain and loss. Not that these things are wrong in themselves. They are quite simply an inadequate foundation that fails to lead to commitment, loyalty and faithfulness. Later we will discover how selfish, opinionated, mean, unkind and even addicted our 'other' is! And they will likely see the same traits in us!

Civil partnership dissolutions soared 28 percent in 2011 (as *The Guardian* revealed in an article in summer 2012). But marriage between men and women has also been under strain and going out of fashion for decades. But surprise, surprise, today more and more people are opting to get married than have done for decades. Also a staggering 600,000 people, including scores of MPs, oppose Prime Minister Cameron's plans to create same-sex marriage. Each signed a Campaign4Marriage petition – the largest government online response ever. Many high-profile gay people do not want same-sex marriages either. They are aware that the increase in same-sex broken relationships have happened in a few short years since the Labour government forced [this] through in 2005. They are happy with the current legislation. Most would not claim to be following Christ.

Love is not a feeling but an action, indeed a lifelong series of actions including getting it wrong, apologising, forgiving, and starting again.

'Love never gives up. Love cares more for others than for self. Love doesn't want what it doesn't have. Love doesn't strut, doesn't have a swelled head, doesn't force itself on others. Isn't always 'me first,' doesn't fly off the handle. Doesn't keep score of the sins of others...' (1 Corinthians 13:3–7, The Message)

The above is, in the main, a list of loving *actions* – irrespective of feelings. Would you rather people only love you when they feel like it or do the right thing by word and behaviour out of respect? I suggest – a dimension of love! The romanticisation of love has often led to a strong physical attraction without foundation.

David was a believer – he once had a girlfriend who he liked and cared for – but fancied a guy. He genuinely thought he was in love. His parents asked him to see me. He was charming and honest and part of a large London church. He had a 'special friend' he had known for a very short time. 'So far we have only kissed' he admitted, 'but I guess we will be having full sex in two or three weeks.' No long-term friendship, getting to know one another – a route that might lead to true, committed, self-denying love. It was simply romance, which led him straight into bed for sex. This, from my experience advising Christian same-sex attracted guys, is quite normal – whereas among Christian guys with girlfriends, it is usually a very much slower route from real friendship, to a physical and then later low-level sexual relationship and rarely pre-marital intercourse. There are few such boundaries with 'Christian' men having sex with men in my research and experience.

I have no doubt gay guys looking for love think a sexual relationship will bind the other person to them (as indeed heterosexuals may conclude). This can happen, but often doesn't.

Any married man will tell you, that a session of fun and passion-filled sex can within no time lead to an argument about in-laws, money, future plans, holidays or friends. Romance and sexual intimacy must not be equated with love. Grace, humility, patience, respect and commitment to one's partner and a desire to enhance the value of that person demands a lot more than romance. Coldplay has a great line in one of their songs, 'Give me real don't give me fake'. That's true whether we are opposite- or same-sex attracted.

Love is the most meaningful emotion known to us – but must not be confused with romance, sexual attraction or a physical relationship. All of these can be important, but do not make a good foundation for a long-term future. In fact, sex apart – everything you can find in marriage can be found in any same or opposite sex, committed relationship. Think about it.

To growing numbers of people, particularly young adults, romance is everything – they are convinced that this will lead to commitment. But sometimes even romance is bypassed, it is just sex– as the inside of any men's public toilet door will tell you. This was the amazing case with the wealthy, famous and gifted singer George Michael – arrested in toilets for soliciting!

Human rights and gay marriage

Theresa May, who was Home Secretary at the time said, ' Put simply it's not right that a couple who love each other, and want to formalise a commitment to each other, should be denied the right to marry.'[8]

However, not only does she not believe what she said, but nor do you or I! Marriage between close relatives who 'love' each other? Incest. A 'loving' man and a 14-year-old infatuated boy? Paedophilia. Between two people already married? Bigamy. How about a teacher and young pupil? Or between minors? Perhaps that was a factor when the Strasbourg-based European Court of Human Rights (not exactly known for its Christian commitment) somewhat surprisingly ruled that same-sex marriages are not a human right.[9] There remains a strong sense among the broad Christian community that at a later stage (despite government protestations) churches will be required to marry same-sex couples (against conscience and scripture) or risk discrimination laws.

It was a very brave Ben Bradshaw MP, the former Culture Secretary and currently a practicing homosexual, who told the *Washington Post* that the attempt to redefine marriage was 'pure politics'.[10] Conservative politician Gary Streeter went to Prime Minister David Cameron in early 2012 and warned him that almost 100 Conservative MPs would oppose such a move. Other MPs commented that they had not had one single letter requesting same-sex marriage! It was a very foolish Lynne Featherstone, the Home Office minister supposedly overseeing the consultation on same-sex marriage, who *The Daily Telegraph* reported as saying that it was about 'how, not whether' the measure should be introduced. So not only was she redefining marriage but redefining what a 'consultation' is!

Once marriage has been redefined it can be whatever groups want it to be. In the USA it remains illegal to have more than one wife – so some men in several States have one legal wife but live with several others. In Canada there are already campaigns for the legalisation of polygamy. It is more than likely that there will be further demands for redesigns.

There are of course different sorts of families, but these are rarely by design. Death, separation, divorce or long-term sickness create pains and pressures – but single parents can be amazing! Yet every survey concludes that traditional one man and one woman marriage is the best environment to bring children up. In January 1999 the Government Green Paper on the family stated that: 'Marriage is still the surest foundation for raising children and remains the choice for the majority of people in Britain. 70% of children in Britain are brought up by married parents.'

Political correctness

'Do you realise how bigoted you are?' is an argument often aimed at anyone with our views.

Currently we are told we live in a modern society, teeming with people who hold quite different views on so many issues. Any of these may be – and sometimes have to be – challenged. Just take a look at Prime Minister's Question Time at the Palace of Westminster. There are rules the Speaker upholds, but it seems at times that almost everything can be challenged with hostility and cheap jibes – and on international television. No one has ever been charged with Tory–phobia, Liberal bigotry or Labour narrow mindedness!

However, the Lesbian, Gay, Bisexual and Transgender spokespeople (LGBT) don't hold with this approach at all. And it matters not a jot to them that many decent homosexuals understand and agree with what you are now reading.

I was one of the founders of an organisation that cares for more people (mainly gay) dying of AIDS in their homes than any other charity. We had many talks with gifted, often very young bright, individuals whose lives were tragically being cut short through accidents or irresponsible behaviour. So, far from being backward or traditional (old-fashioned) we are actually progressives as we look into the future. The brilliant singer/songwriter Sir Elton John said of his adopted son Zachery that, 'It's going to be heart-breaking for him to grow up and realise he hasn't got a Mummy'.[11] A wise and insightful public statement worthy of reflection.

An organisation that is not willing to be scrutinised is not modern at all. Somebody commented that the LGBT movement is working to construct the same kind of society in which it was once so unwelcome.

Section 28 of the Local Government Act 1988 remains controversial. This law says that public money must not be spent promoting homosexuality, especially in schools. Nevertheless, the academic research organisation Christian Institute traced £1 million of public money diverted from education and health to promote gay rights and homosexuality. And this was after a mere three weeks of research, 'the tip of an iceberg'! [12]. Most parents have little or no idea what their children are taught about sexuality at school. And some of the educational elite really do believe 'teacher knows best'.

Money that should be spent on education and treating sick people is in defiance of the law, normalising people of the same sex having sex.

Section 28 states that:

1. 'A local authority shall not intentionally promote homosexuality or publish material with the intention of promoting homosexuality';

2. [Or] 'promote the teaching in any maintained school of the acceptability of homosexuality as a pretended family relationship.'

Young people, particularly boys, often go through a stage (or stages) of experiencing same-sex attraction and inquisitiveness, but most grow out of it. This stage should not be exploited.

Homosexual behaviour also carries significant risks to health. Anal intercourse can be particularly hazardous. The UK's National Blood Service bans anyone who has engaged in this activity in the previous 12 months from giving blood. Across Europe and North America it is a life-time ban.

HIV and AIDS

So what is this final heading doing in a chapter about homosexuality? We all know that HIV/AIDS is a global phenomenon that hits men and women, children of both sexes and even babies.

Quite right – but stay with me!

HIV is the Human Immunodeficiency Virus and infections occur mainly in two high-risk groups – men having anal unprotected sex with men (MSM), and unprotected vaginal or anal heterosexual penetration. The virus is present in saliva, urine, sperm and blood – but it is diluted, so you cannot be infected through kissing or sitting on a toilet seat for example. It is normally passed on through the rich secretions that are present in penetrative sex.

AIDS is the Acquired Immune Deficiency Syndrome that follows HIV, and which eventually breaks down the body's defences against illness. Use of condoms provides safer sex (not safe sex). There are tiny holes in the latex material, invisible to the eye, that can cause the condom to split in use, or slip off an erect or flaccid penis.

Safe sex only occurs between a virgin enjoying sex (in a committed relationship) with another virgin.

Below are informed estimates, published by UNAIDS,

WHO and UNICEF in November 2011, that refer to the end of 2010 (this is because global figures take a long time to gather, collate and publish).

This is a limited survey covering aspects of the disease. Further exhaustive statistics are available for many countries at www.Avert.org

Worldwide 34 million people were HIV positive at the close of 2010.
In 2010 alone there were 1.8 million AIDS-related deaths.
There were 2.7 million newly infected people.
Since the early 80s, 30 million have died from AIDS.

In Western Europe 840,000 are infected with HIV.
In 2010 there were 30,000 new infections.

In the UK there were 86,500 living with HIV, 25% unaware they were infected.
In 2010 there were 6,136 diagnosed new HIV infections.
26,791 have so far been diagnosed with full-blown AIDS.
19,912 of those diagnosed have died.
London has 28,000 recorded HIV infections.

In the UK, covering all years to December 2010 those diag-nosed with HIV include:
Men having sex with men (MSM) 50,137
Heterosexuals 51,378
Those on drugs/sharing needles 5,396

I have included these statistics in part to reveal that here in the UK the number of gay men having sex is a fraction of the heterosexual population doing the same. Yet the numbers of those infected is almost identical. This can only mean many more same-sex partners and/or high-risk activity. We have lost a lot of very gifted guys due to a lack of care, education and understanding.
    Due to state-of-the-art medications AIDS in the developed

world is no longer a death sentence but a chronic disease. But there remains no cure for AIDS.

So, as we have discovered, same-sex attraction leading to same-sex activity can have devastating results. Our aim is to provide understanding, care and support. All of us are sexually deficient and flawed and all of us need the Holy Spirit and scripture to point us back to Calvary where Christ paid the ultimate price to enable us to live a life that's pleasing to Him.

Having strong feelings for someone isn't love – it is romanticism and is often deceptive. If we choose to do the right biblical thing then the right feelings often follow. If we feed affections and emotions through fantasy or porn then we are playing with fire.

Doing the hardest thing and the right thing...is often the same thing!

'I do not see why we need to change the law, especially at this time when there are so many other important matters for the Government to be addressing.'

Tim Loughton,
Minister for Children and Families.

Notes

1. Evelyn Beatrice Hall, *The Friends of Voltaire*, 1906
2. *Pink News*, 23 May 2012
3. 'New Testament Scandals', *Christianity* magazine, 2009
4. In recent years scientific papers have proposed a 'gay gene theory' but the wider scientific community has rejected all of these. In 1993 professor Dean Hamer announced that he had found the 'gay gene'. Two years later a member of his own staff voiced doubts about this theory and was sacked (covered in *The Times* 10 July 1995) In 1999, after a two year study looking into his claims, scientists in Canada concluded there was no basis for Hamer's conclusions, *Science*, April 23 1999

5. *Queerbychoice.com*
6. Merlin Holland, *The Real Trial of Oscar Wilde*
7. *The Times*, 21 April 2012
8. *The Daily Telegraph*, 17 June 2012
9. *Daily Mail*, 8 June 2012
10. Campaign for Marriage, 3.4.2012
11. *Mail Online*, 15 June 2012
12. Colin Hart, Christian Institute, 11 November 1989

Chapter 5

The Vital R Word

Gerald: None of us are wired for rejection, hate, ridicule or loneliness. We are wired for the exact opposite!

But events take place, words are spoken, we can get left out of groups for no apparent reason... We can be overlooked for promotion and, despite busyness, important relationships, responsibilities and goals, can often feel we are very much on our own. We all *need* to be loved and to love others. But we have all become damaged by external circumstances and bad choices, some made because of what is going on in our own hearts and minds.

Feeling disconnected, and maybe unheard and under-valued, we can turn inwards, and sometimes, especially if we are guys, to porn. This is often because we are looking for comfort and pleasure. We are on the road to substitutionary fulfilment. Porn provides immediate gratification, but not relationships. Ah there it is – the R word – relationships! But so often we decide that relationships can be too costly and painful. So we end up, at least in part, living primarily for our own enjoyment, not for others and certainly not to please God.

As Timothy Keller wrote of Adam before Eve '...even in paradise, loneliness was a terrible thing.'[1]

A young friend of mine was getting depressed about his laptop visits in his bedroom. Then he met a girl and for several months he never typed in the words that led to anticipation, excitement and brief, ultimately unfulfilling, pleasure. Why? He had a healthy, helpful relationship, so didn't need porn! Then they hit misunderstandings, recriminations and separated. Alas there were few informed, mutual friends to advise, support and pray. The laptop suddenly reappeared, taking him back down a route of depression and self-disgust. But an older father figure took some initiative, my friend made his confession and he was guided back to freedom. Thank God for broad, trustworthy, open relationships!

God is relational

Can you imagine that on one occasion, God made something that wasn't good? Well that's what scripture states. Having had what can only be described as an orgy of pure fun and power, creating galaxies, planets, stars, suns and moons – God turns His attention to one wandering star, which is what the word planet means. We call it earth! There followed light, sky. Plants, trees and fruit. More lights, times and seasons, fish, birds, animals and then...His masterpiece! A person like Him, to be in charge of it all. For that person, He created a garden, rivers, more trees and fruit – it was paradise!

Then God looked again, 'It's not good for the Man to be alone; I'll make him a helper, a companion'. (Genesis 2:18, The Message) Why couldn't Adam reflect the image of God without Eve? Because God, the Godhead, is community. God the Father, God the Son and God the Holy Spirit. They were, and remain, a community of love, commitment, mercy, grace, truth, happiness and fun. They respect and care about each other, believe in each other, support each other – and none acts independently of the other. They are in everything together. They are permanently accountable, transparent, harmonious and affectionate.

And that is how we are designed to be – relational, just like our Creator.

We cannot walk in everyone else's shoes. That is the route to a breakdown. But we can learn from the Godhead. We can learn to walk in *their* shoes. And that will undoubtedly bless those in other shoes...

I do it because I'm lonely

John lived in a town near to us. He was part of a good church – but it was resistant to new ways of doing things and somewhat formal. He heard what was happening in our small, but slowly growing church. He started to come over and soon realised he had 'come home'!

One sunny day he told me he had some 'private' things to share. So we went out for a drive and stopped in a layby in the country. 'I have something to tell you', he confided. I waited with baited breath, wondering what he had done. His story unfolded. Despite having a good, healthy and stable family, a reasonable education and friends he was in trouble. 'I have been masturbating, often several times a day', he confessed with shame. Everyone who knew him thought he was amazing with a bright future. None were aware of what he was hiding. Then he visited our church, confessed to me and moved house to be part of the church community. 'In no time at all this compulsion evaporated', he later explained, 'and all because of meaningful, open relationships. I am a completely different person, with no current secrets, cover-ups or lies.'

Yes we were made for relationships, for sharing our lives with others. We were not made for isolation, not even 'just me and God' – unless you are overseas, being persecuted for your faith and in prison! And we were not made simply to work together. Such relationships in the workplace, and even church, come and go and within hardly any time at all they are quite simply a distant memory.

What was 'normal' for John was gone; there was no 'normal' to go back to! It was a long time later that he told me, with lip-smacking relish, of how his addiction had become a good news story he could share with others.

Meteorologists have named drought 'the creeping disease'. Huge weather pattern changes, such as floods, storms and sometimes devastating lightning flashes, ferocious winds, hurricanes and tornadoes strike without warning but droughts invade and develop in slow motion day after day, week after week, month after month and hinder the growth of anything healthy, fruitful and nutritious. This is how it is without deep, open, meaningful friendships and relationships. We get isolated, plain busy and even so locked up that our partners and children can't reach us. So I say it again, apart from sex, almost everything else you can find in marriage can be found in other relationships. God has so blessed relational single people!

Position and condition

Once you have heard and responded to the good news of Christ, which offers forgiveness for the past, cleansing for the present and hope for the future, you have a new position, relationally and universally. Christ dying for the sin and wrongdoing of us all changes everything. (Someone some-where has to pay the price for criminal activity – the judge of the earth cannot just wink and say 'It doesn't matter'.) Yes this changes everything – and changes you. The old position was one where we were lost, in darkness, sin and even outright rebellion against God Himself. It was not a good position to face Christ in.

Now your position has changed, you are a 'son of God' – whether you are male or female. The theme of sonship is worthy of a book within itself, let me explain. When we gave our lives to Christ (and you may yet need to) you received His offer of forgiveness and a new start. In a sense you were born again, spiritually. And as such you became a child, not of earthly parents but a heavenly Father.

John, who was Jesus' best friend, understood this well:

People conceived and brought into life by God don't make a practice of sin. How could they? God's seed is deep within them, making them who they are. It's not in the nature of the God-begotten to practice and parade sin. Here's how you tell the difference between God's children and the Devil's children: The one who won't practice righteous ways isn't from God, nor is the one who doesn't love brother and sister. A simple test. (1 John 3:9–10, The Message)

Wow! John doesn't exactly pull his punches does he? He is not talking about occasional failures, even regular, low-level damaging failures – but someone who *'won't'* live for Christ as a son, but may even call themselves Christian! But do you see how John relates our new *position* (sonship) to our new, daily, developing *condition*. (The alternative is a life of personal sin and refusing to love God's people – the Church!) As I am no longer in darkness, sin and rebellion I am open to God the Holy Spirit, to Creation itself, to scripture and relationships. This understanding of who I am (identity) gives me a new position and thus affects my daily, ongoing, condition. I choose to live as a son of God, living in the light of Calvary, no longer in the darkness and decay, corruption or self-inflicted damage of the past. And this includes past sexual relationships!

Because of Calvary, our future does not have to be a re-run of our history!

And did you notice, John finishes with what he considers a 'simple test' – relationships of love. Our new position affects our condition and results in loving relationships. Also, remember what we wrote about love: it is a series of actions that may not always be matched by warm or exciting feelings.

The power of accountability

As I sit here today, writing this in Leatherhead, Surrey, England, I am aware that in a short time, there will be thousands of readers, like you, across the UK, Continental Europe, North America, Australia and New Zealand, and maybe other nations and peoples. For some you will be reading in your garden (back yards for our American friends!) Some will be on holiday, in Bible schools, at the workplace, in a lunch break or privately reading in their bedrooms. I am thinking of you – Nathan and I have prayed for you. Nearing the end of the book, how can we help you stay on course?

I have had a rule in life, which has pretty much kept me on the straight and narrow. The rule is – if I am asked a question about the nature of a friendship, how much I eat, or drink, when I last viewed porn, maybe how much I have paid for something, or various things I may have said or done – to ask myself if I would tell a lie. If the answer is yes then I am doing wrong!

One guy I know, while at university, was staying overnight in his girlfriend's bedroom, sharing the same bed. They did everything other than penetrative sex. But he was convinced they weren't having sex. 'Then why do you creep out of the house at the crack of dawn?' I enquired. 'Have you told your parents or her parents? Maybe you have told your pastor, CU leader or a close friend? 'They wouldn't understand', he replied. Here he was not only lying to his girlfriend and anyone who dared ask – but was being dishonest with himself.

During the August 2012 Olympics, one Gold Medal winner is reported to have tweeted on the night of his victory that he was utterly and totally drunk, out of his head. The next morning the national press reported he had been seen in what amounted to a sex club. He was convinced there was nothing wrong with either – in fact he boasted about it all.

Compare that to Long Jump Gold Medal winner Greg Rutherford. (I am not aware he is a committed Christian, unlike many medallists and competitors). He explained, having won his medal, that four years previously he had experienced a bad time because his grandfather had died. But then gave thanks for his 'brilliant' parents and amazing girlfriend. It seemed as if he had made himself accountable to them all. I sensed he felt he owed them something. And I doubt whether it included drinking beer until he was legless or looking for sex with a complete stranger! It was so refreshing to hear him. But it was relationships that had made him different from the other medallist.

Turning back to the writing of this book, it took Nathan and me over four months to finish the manuscript and send it off to the publisher – this was amidst many other respon-sibilities. Prior to and during that time, I asked him many questions about sexuality, spirituality and past relationships. (It is how we came to write this book in the first place.) I knew that at any time he could ask the same of me and espe-cially whether, as we wrote about sex, wanking, porn and stories of addiction, I had succumbed to looking at porn. My wife Anona was even more likely to ask the same of me. I owed it to them both, out of warm love and deep respect, for that answer to be 'no'. And so it was and remains. I made myself accountable to them, though they never knew that explicitly.

Our secret actions are usually our most shameful – and can bring people that are in leadership positions into disre-pute, despite a long history of consistency and accountability. If the press were to discover such things, many friends, readers and listeners would be disappointed, angry and could even stumble in their commitment to Christ. That is also constantly in my mind, making me accountable.

In closing this chapter, we shall see that scripture puts a high premium on relationships.

'Just as lotions and fragrance give sensual delight, a sweet friendship refreshes the soul.' (Proverbs 27:9–10, The Message)

'You use steel to sharpen steel, and one friend sharpens another.' (Proverbs 27:17, The Message)

'Friends love through all kinds of weather.' (Proverbs 17:17, The Message)

Perhaps one of the most staggering moments in Christ's ministry is when Judas arrives to betray Him. He kisses Jesus, who then says, 'Friend, why this charade?' (Matthew 26:50, The Message) Judas was not Christ's friend, but, even at this moment, Jesus calls him friend.

Sometimes we find friendships develop into charitable

work, improving the lives of others at home or abroad. Sometimes we simply work alongside people and in so doing we become long-term friends and even confidantes. Friendship can bring opposites together and provide a common purpose.

But to experience the fun and joy of deep and lasting friendship, we have to give up the 'I know best mentality', which usually leads to no friends at all!

'True friends stab you in the front.'
Oscar Wilde

Notes

1. Tim Keller, *The Meaning of Marriage,* Hodder and Stoughton.

Chapter 6

Be Protected

pro·tect
Verb (used with object)

To defend or guard from attack, invasion, loss, annoyance, insult, etc.; cover or shield from injury or danger.

Nathan: The very nature of the word protect reveals that it's a verb. It is not a solid state. It is not a ticked box. It is ever ready, prepared, moving. It is always adapting and changing how we operate. On the journey of freedom we need protection; just as our addictive behaviour has affected every area of our life, so must our protection. This is protection from temptation, potential actions, lifestyles and thinking. It is not simply a list of barriers and guards to put up, but a renewed mind and lifestyle that doesn't just help us stay protected but encourages and strengthens our faith and journey.

Isn't God our protector? Won't He watch our back? Yes, God is our protector. But there are steps we must take in our thinking, feeling and doing to set us well under the protection He provides. So how are we working toward applying the attribute of God the Protector to our lives?

A person can discover the safest tower with the best security, but if they don't know how to enter, and if they don't stay inside, they cannot benefit from it, regardless of how long they may speak of it, see it and be drawn to it. I hope that this chapter helps you develop the keys I discovered to enter into God's protection and stay there for good.

The journey onward and upward

A journey is never going to lead you to new sights and experiences if, on that journey, you walk backward. We are human. We will mess up at some point. When we do make a mistake, however large or small, we do not need to return to the beginning of our journey. The mistake may halt us, but it will never lessen our eternal worth or the call on our lives. Our sin may pause us but it is our choice to step back further or continue on our journey forward. That said, how do we prevent ourselves from walking backward? How do we continue journeying onward into a fulfilling life for Christ?

In my own life, one of the reasons it took me so long to walk in freedom is because I didn't place boundaries in the three key target areas that make up how we live: thinking, feeling and doing. I failed and there was nothing stopping me from stepping backward.

Failure would be like landing on a snake in a game of snakes and ladders, but with each snake on my board leading me right back to the beginning of the journey. It is easy to forget that the game is rigged, fixed, for our lives. Through the freedom and forgiveness Jesus gave us we never have to go down the snakes when we land on them: we will always land on spaces that we can move forward from.

> 'No temptation has overtaken you except such as is common to man; but God is faithful, who will not allow you to be tempted beyond what you are able, but with the temptation will also make the way of escape, that you may be able to bear it.' (1 Corinthians 10:13, NKJV)

Our lives will always have temptations and trials; the snake will always be there to lead us back into our old habits and cycles. However, there are ways in which we can behave to be protected from this temptation. We can choose not to turn in certain directions. We have the choice to move forward. We have the choice to journey toward places where we will be surrounded, not by snakes, but by ladders. These ladders lead us into a deeper relationship with God, to a new revelation, momentum of faith and obedience to His word. We must create a level of discipline, under the freedom of grace and in the truth of our identity. We must continually give our lives the option not to enter into the same self-destructive cycle, but into new productive ones. We can culti-vate cycles, systems and habits that will lead us to a deepening of our relationship with Him and a further clarity of His call for our lives. Ladders are an upward climb and they can be hard to contend with. However, falling a few rungs is much less destructive than falling back to the beginning of the journey. We must climb, not crawl, into our full, free, lives.

'I in them and you in me – so that they may be brought to complete unity.' (John 17:23, NIV)

God wants to be in our lives completely. Connected through His Son, God wants there to be no gap between Him and us, so that we would not simply know of God but be restored to live with Him. We can build a life that treasures Him. The ladders are there. God has created systems through his Son and Spirit that enable us to enter into a deeper rela-tionship with Him, not just a 'closer' relationship (His Spirit lives inside of us, how much closer can that be?) Usually those ladders will take effort to find, humility to confront and faith to climb. They are vital, though, in protecting us as they lead us deeper into God. They create ways in which we can further embrace Him through highlighting where we need to change, challenging us to make the change and giving a way for us to do so. Those ladders can be people we need to talk to, things we need to commit to and, perhaps, even reading this book. In my experience the most effective ladders we can climb are the ones God has shown us. These ladders are uniquely placed in our lives, tailored to who we are and what God wants for us as individuals. These are the ladders that sin can so often hide from us, or cause us to ignore or misun-derstand.

Where are you going?

Another key into understanding how we can be fused to God's protection is the direction our lives are heading in. What we are aiming for? What do we want our lives to look like? Where do we want to see ourselves in a week, a month or a year's time? What are the dreams we have and what 'good works' do we want to do for God?

The Christian's intention and direction should be based on loving Him and loving others. This forms markers that we live by and head toward. There are unique things placed on our lives from God that make up who we are, and these are what the devil corrupts and attempts to destroy. The specificity of how you love God and how you love others is important. The destruction of this is the destruction of the unique path and direction you can use to journey further into fulfilling your life with His purpose.

In my mind I had become what I was doing so I felt I was identified by my sin, not by my standing as a child of God. We can become disconnected as to why we are here, because our worth becomes so minute. I decided my worth was my usefulness, which was a dangerous place to be, because what I felt I was useful for lessened and lessened each time I failed to fight my problems. I felt useless, a waste of resources to my family and to the rest of the world. I could do no good.

If we feel we have no worth we feel we have no use. When writing this I tried to think of a worthless material. I concluded that ash is probably the most useless material, however even ash can be turned into a diamond, something that is seen as one of the most precious things on earth. This is quite a good metaphor of what God does with our seemingly worthless lives. He takes the worthless and creates worth by our ability to channel and reflect the Light of the world. Reading and applying the truth of our worth means the acknowledgment and outworking that we also have purpose. By reconnecting with our worth we reconnect with what we can be useful for by seeing ourselves in the way that

God sees us – irreplaceably precious.

During the lowest times of my life I didn't see any usefulness in myself because I was looking too specifically for a perfect calling. It stopped me from doing anything, so I began to stagnate. I lost touch with what the purpose of my life was, in search for who I should become. I became isolated from the person that gave my life purpose (God) and the people that would have shown me that truth. In that isolation, disconnection and disillusionment a dangerous lie was cultivated: 'there is no unique calling for you'. By crawling out of my stagnation and reconnecting to God and others, I discovered where I was going wrong. I discovered that we all have the same base calling as Christians, to love God and love others. What sets us apart and gives us the keys in fulfilling that calling, is how we as individuals shape it through the uniqueness of who we are, and who God wants us to be.

We will never find out in what way we are commissioned if we never commit to doing whatever we can to meet the overall call. As you understand the unique way that you meet the call on your life to love God and love others, you can then shape more specifically what you want to do to continue to meet that. What you are more gifted at and what you really enjoy doing will be the way you should love others and God. This direction and discovery will always bring us closer to God as we seek to love Him through what we do. It is one more step in placing our lives well under His protection.

You must hold on, and stay connected, to your identity in Christ, the gifts, talents and tools God has given you. Outworking who we are in God brings us under His protection. In order to do this for myself I wrote down what I was good at, what my dreams were and what I wanted my life to look like. By doing this I had things to aspire to and work toward. Things that I knew I could only reach through disowning the dysfunctional family of sin. We only get out of bed because we have a reason to; without a reason to stop sinning we will still sin. Even if it is a simple declaration of, 'I want to be in a deeper relationship with God, free from pornography and wanking.' If we are dwelling with that each day and putting ourselves around people who will support us on that journey, we will have a greater chance of remembering where we want to be and staying on track to get there.

Free connections

In Jewish law, in order to be purified after an impure act or impurity, you would have to follow specific laws and regulations so you could be welcomed back into the community. These laws, in the most basic of terms, involved someone clean helping cleanse the unclean. We don't live under Old Testament Law, however looking at the way that purification took place in that historical and cultural context can help us remain protected once we have been made pure.

None of us are pure without God. We are stained with our past and our present mistakes. Through the death and resurrection of Jesus Christ we know that He gave us a way out of our mistakes. Through dying with every wrong, and then living again without them, Jesus paid the price for our sin. He gave us a way we can live lives of purity where we can ask Him to remove our wrongdoing. Under Jewish law you could not be cleansed without the help of someone who was already clean, just as we cannot be clean without Him. We cannot be pure if we are disconnected from the source of purity. The temptation is to isolate ourselves because of how dirty and seemingly helpless we feel. I felt I couldn't talk to anyone, couldn't go to anyone with my problems. I felt as if I couldn't even approach God anymore. However we must fight against those feelings, we must break through the prison of our faulty mind-sets and reach out to the place where our freedom comes from and remember we are inseparable from Him under salvation.

Being protected is being inseparable from the One who protects us. We can strive as much as we want to have full freedom without Him, but even if the sister problems are ignored and overcome practically, the effects they have had on our lives cannot be reversed through mental strength alone. The problem is that the effect of porn and its sister is not simply momentary, but cancerous in the way it affects our lives. So a complete removal of not simply the resulting behaviour, but a controlling of the triggers, the thought process and the spiritual response, needs to happen. God alone holds the power to overcome all the effects that plague our life. He has the authority over all the spiritual aspects, another key into the full coverage of His protection.

'For God did not appoint us to wrath, but to obtain salvation through our Lord Jesus Christ, who died for us, that whether we wake or sleep, we should live together with Him.' (1 Thessalonians 5:9–10, NKJV)

The very purpose in the freedom that Christ provides is for us to be able to enter into a relationship with the holy, mighty and just Father. He gave us the way we could come before the dangerous King. Without it we would simply be obliterated by the sheer power and holiness that He exudes. The freedom was not simply a gift but a key in allowing us to face God. The very nature of the freedom and forgiveness is to bring us to meet and be in relationship with Him, to be called His child! The two work as one, freedom simply being one of the attributes as He lives in us. To be free we need Him, and freedom is in Him.

To hold onto freedom is to hold onto God; the moment we let go of God, we let go of freedom. The rope pulls us the same way, to seek after one and not the other is to misunderstand freedom and neglect God. Another key to protection is the application of freedom and forgiveness as the gate to God, putting it to its full use. Seeking a relationship with God, having freedom and forgiveness of our sins, does not only grant us everlasting life but encourages us to transform the life we have now. We can benefit today from the acceptance He has given us through resurrection and the connection we have through His Spirit. We are not free after we have reached a certain level of relationship with God; we are free in order to live with Him each and every day.

Distinctly different

The Israelites were God's people. They were chosen and special, a holy nation, and their name literally meant 'bright and set apart'. This enabled them to fulfil their special purpose as a people; they had laws that enabled them to do so. God's favour and love we know is now available to all; anyone can enter into a loving relationship with Christ. We no longer live under law but grace. We are no longer under Old Testament Law; Jesus fulfilled the Law. We are, however, still called to be, and have been made, holy – not by law but by forgiveness and the indwelling of the Holy Spirit.

The pursuit of holiness is one of the greatest forms of protection. It is a direct choice to acknowledge God has made us holy and live our lives in accordance to that holiness. This is fully accepting that the only way we can maintain our protection is by being connected to the Protector. We can place all our effort into living closer dedication to Him. Protection is cultivated as we work toward setting our thinking, feeling and doing to be ruled by God. To maintain holy lives we must aim to live like the holy one.

'As obedient children, let yourselves be pulled into a way of life shaped by God's life, a life energetic and blazing with holiness. God said, "I am holy; you be holy."' (1 Peter 1:14–16, The Message)

We must live lives 'shaped by God' if we want to really see a complete removal and reversal of the problems, lives that bring control and protection from the potential temptation triggers. We must live set apart. We are in, but not of, the world. Transforming the way we live our lives, one step at a time, is to align with our purpose, identity and aspirations. If I want to be like Jesus, I will look at His life and look at mine to discover what I need to change to bring my thoughts and intentions in line with His own. We can often become so intertwined with the systems and the ways in which the world works that we go through the conventional practice of life without giving a second thought to it.

We have been made holy, we are saved, but not by anything we do! As much as our spirit has been made holy, victorious and free, the rest of who we are is not. We can still live for our flesh, be more attracted and lured by the world, despite the Holy Spirit living inside of us.

> 'For those who live according to the flesh set their minds on the things of the flesh, but those who live according to the Spirit, the things of the Spirit. For to be carnally minded [ruled by the flesh] is death, but to be spiritually minded is life and peace.' (Romans 8:5–6, NKJV)

We must make the conscious choice to be ruled not by our bodily desires but by our spiritual yearning for more of God. We are able to strengthen our spiritual desire and ambition above all else, to 'live according to the Spirit'. This is easier said than done. But God protects us through providing a different way to live. Through conquering sin and death and sending his Spirit, we can live spiritually minded lives. Lives that don't need to surrender to the temptations of this world, but through Him have the power and strength to overcome whatever we may face...and then to receive the fruit of what living by His Spirit provides.

Thought mastery

Living life according to the Holy Spirit ultimately boils down to what choices we make – and remembering we have them in the first place. It is up to us to decide to live by the Holy Spirit. In some ways it was simpler for the Israelites, to listen and follow what God said and remain His children. Today we don't have that quasi point system that existed, but instead we have grace and a love for God and others. Grace, love and a desire to be governed by the Holy Spirit are so important. So what does that look like practically? How do we commit to that? Knowing that I failed in my struggle by not placing barriers in those three key areas I can now target them: thinking, feeling and doing.

The battle starts in our thinking and is won by our actions. If we give spiritual thinking power over carnal thinking then we give spiritual living victory over carnal choices.

'For the weapons of our warfare are not carnal but mighty in God for pulling down strongholds, casting down arguments and every high thing that exalts itself against the knowledge of God, bringing every thought into captivity to the obedience of Christ, and being ready to punish all disobedience when your obedience is fulfilled.' (2 Corinthians 10:4–6, NKJV)

If we hold our thoughts captive and bring them under control we can do the same with our choices. While I was struggling with the issues I faced I often entered into a 'default' mode. I would live under automated responses, not shaped by scripture but by feelings and wants. The realisation of the choices made and their consequences would only hit me after the deed was done. I had little or no control over my thinking so my actions followed suit. The Message translation of the above scripture makes what we need to do even clearer: 'fitting every loose thought and emotion and impulse into the structure of life shaped by Christ.' That's exactly what we must do; learn to stop and analyse our thinking and how we are feeling.

We must learn to ask: 'does this align with the truth of God's word and what He says about me?' Here's an example of the type of thinking that causes undesired action: 'I've messed up already, I can't be used for anything because of this problem so I may as well do it since it makes me feel good.' We may not consciously say that, but, if we stopped to think, that may be what is in our head. So we must learn to stop and ask ourselves what is going on in our head. We always have the choice to do that. We can then take the time to think about the truth that we live under and combat the lie with that truth. But this requires us to read the Bible, something I will come onto later.

Once the error of our thinking is singled out we can then recognise and replace it with the truth. It can be helpful to say something like: 'Devil, you have no power over me and I rebuke your lies. I am loved and my purpose is to love. I have messed up, but I have been forgiven through Christ paying for my sin'. This is when our actions support our thinking, so instead of meeting with the evil sisters we meet with heaven and literally avenge our thinking, which is the literal translation of the word 'punish' in the passage from 2 Corinthians.10:6.

This methodology is not new. Jesus combated temptation in the same way, through knowing the truth of scripture. It is even better when we know what the Bible says for ourselves. That is why I quote scripture, so that it can be taken and used in battle.

Dwelling on scripture is a sure fire way of guarding our minds and staying protected. In fact, the Bible tells us precisely what to dwell on. If we continually dwell on sex, we will see things through that lens and so be further tempted. However, if we dwell on the things the Bible guides us to, we will see things through Christ's perspective.

'Whatever things are true, whatever things are noble, whatever things are just, whatever things are pure, whatever things are lovely, whatever things are of good report, if there is any virtue and if there is anything praiseworthy – meditate on these things.' (Philippians 4:8, NKJV)

No one wants to be burnt by fire, but often we can think that we can dwell on whatever we want to in our minds and remain unaffected. However the likelihood is that you will be burnt if you are playing with the very thing you don't want to be affected by. If we don't want to be burnt by sin we need to be engulfed in living waters.

Holy decorum

> 'You are a chosen generation, a royal priesthood, a holy nation, His own special people, that you may proclaim the praises of Him who called you out of darkness into His marvellous light.' (1 Peter 2:9, NKJV)

We are royalty, so we must not only think like holy royalty, holding our thoughts captive, but we must live like royalty. In Colossians 3:12–14 it says that since we are the 'elect' or 'chosen' of God we must 'clothe' ourselves with 'kindness, humility, meekness, longsuffering, forgiving one another... and love'; in other words we must dress the part and act the part. If we are seeking to remain protected through the pursuit of holiness we must live bright and be set apart.

It is easy to misconceive holiness as isolation, and this has been by different groups over the years. But another metaphor we have is salt and light (Matthew 5:12–17). I would say that light is not isolated from darkness, it is right there in the thick of it – but is not affected by it. In reality it changes the darkness around it, affecting its environment. We need not condone all non-Christian practice as sinful, but instead restore its original intent and purpose, making our behaviour irresistible to others as we reflect Christ. So how does this protect us? Through living our lives as salt and light we affect the 'fashion' and activities of the world, while we ourselves endeavour to remain unaffected. We speak up on how things should be, being examples in our gifting and profession rather than simply slipping into the movements of day-to-day life.

Because of God's immense generosity and grace, we don't have to dissect and scrutinise every action to see if it will pass muster. But the point is not to just get by. We want to live well, but our foremost efforts should be to help others live well.

Selflessness not selfishness should define our actions. Are we edifying ourselves and the body of Christ, or are we simply seeking to entertain our flesh? If we know certain actions trigger a certain response it is wiser to not engage with the action than to abuse or misuse grace. Acts 20:32 states that grace is to 'build us up'. Our actions should point to God's character, either through our actions or how we do them.

One action that cannot be missed is our personal devotions, alone, in small group and/or gathered church. These allow us to personally identify with and know the scriptures, to learn the art of surrender and humility while being challenged and encouraged to fervently run the race marked out. They can create openness to share and deal with problems and be training grounds for the implementation of our battle plans. In these focused times we also discover what our weapons are and when they are best suited to our situations. In addition, prayer and worship should be pivotal in our actions. They teach us to surrender before God, so we can be open around others.

The Holy Spirit is the backbone of being protected. It is the prompting of the truth and the power to apply it that is all-important. We discover the knowledge of what the Kingdom coming looks like and the connection to the King. It is the overwhelming channel of love and the confidence in His calling. If we indeed want to live with Him, we must use our time accordingly, to remain with Him. What better way of practicing than to equip ourselves with the armour God provides each day, consciously running through the importance of each piece, its purpose and what it protects (see Ephesians 6:11–20).

Protection from sin is ultimately cultivating a way of thinking and living that is both inseparable from God and acts as a catalyst for bringing ourselves and others closer to Him.

'Being free means "being free for the other", because the other has bound me to him. Only in relationship with the other am I free.'

Dietrich Bonhoeffer in Creation and Fall

Chapter 7

What About the GF?

Gerald: This book is not primarily about boy/girl friendships or girlfriends, however we felt it would be remiss of us if we finished without mentioning either. Firstly because you may have a girlfriend – or have had several – or secondly you hope to have one sometime.

Most Christian guys still in education know that a girlfriend is often comforting and fun but also a distraction, sometimes a massive temptation and is likely to provide a 'hope deferred makes the heart grow sick' (Proverbs 13:12) scenario. That is, you will eventually finish school and college, possibly go to university and, if you do, come out in your early/mid-20s unsure of a job (even with good qualifications), and loaded with considerable debt. The average age of a guy getting married these days is 29 years and a woman 27 years. This is primarily related to income, debt and job security and issues of geography, parents and church. This means that these guys (as our stories reveal) have been exposed to porn for well over ten years! So do you tell the girlfriend?

I am always amazed that sometimes after just a few weeks or months into a relationship, couples are sharing their sexual histories, going into some detail about previous physical involvements. And all this is shared without a commitment to marriage and lifelong loyalty and faithfulness! But guys rarely mention years of regular and even frequent porn and wanking...

I know of several youth groups in which guys have started dating and these confessions of previous physical involvement have been shared, sometimes in the hope that what was encouraged or allowed in former relationships would start in their current one. Instead of a firewall going up whatever barrier was there is virtually removed. If a girl sexed-up a former boyfriend, or a guy was allowed to go as far as he wanted – then why not now? And if this all takes place in the youth group or church, and things don't work out, it is likely that you will be on the list of guys who have 'done stuff'. And that sure affects a youth group or church!

We also have the problem that dating is not found in scripture. Indeed we are told to treat the sisters (in the church) as sisters in 1 Timothy 5:2. So how far would you go with your sister? But I can already hear your incredulous question: 'isn't that just old-fashioned'? If that's the case does the Bible have anything whatsoever to say to this crucial stage (often lasting years in the dating scenario)? If not, that leaves us to our own devices, which means we sometimes ignore conscience and the Holy Spirit.

I do know of guys who have a healthy relationship with a girlfriend. Often they decide to talk out the nature of the special friendship early on, discussing how to strengthen the firewall and often forgo university. It is my view that university can sometimes be a virtual waste of time and money for some guys, as they finish three years of studying media or history and then go into a completely different vocation!

Long-term and often long-distance romances are fraught with short-term intensity and therefore temptation. Most guys I have counselled remember the name of every girlfriend and their low-level sexual encounters with them and often use the images as porn when wanking. I did say to one guy that he shouldn't live in the past but I obviously didn't explain what I meant well as his response was, 'But Gerald – the past lives in ME!'

But the 'start young, get married soon' couples are few and far between. So what does a guy do in his late teens or twenties when it comes to girls? Your problem maybe that you feel hot and randy and ready to go – or the opposite – nearing your sell-by-date!

Well, we feel we can do no better than point you to the

early 2013 publication *The Dating Dilemma* by the fantastic Rachel Gardner (who once called me an 'icon'!). Published by IVP, in it she deals with boy/girl relationships being intentionally Christ focused, character forming and deals with what she calls, 'a theology of dating'.

Much more needs to be said about these issues than there is space for here, and Rachel will do better than we can. Founder of The Romance Academy she has for some time spoken in schools, colleges and universities as well as Christian youth events. Her book is well worth a buy and suitable for both sexes. It is biblical, sensible and easily understood.

'We are more sinful and flawed in ourselves than we ever dared believe, yet at the very same time we are more loved and accepted in Jesus Christ than we ever dared hope.'

Timothy and Kathy Keller

Chapter 8

So is M the Answer?

Gerald: No, this book is not primarily about marriage either! But, again, we are aware that many married men will read this. So here are a few words from us before we again recommend a publication that deals with this issue in far greater depth.

However, just to be clear, the M this time *is* marriage!

So one day, two people meet, are drawn to each other, fall in love, get married and hope it will last forever. That is how it has been for hundreds of generations. But today, the array of opposition is immense.

First, there are the modern pressures of adjusting to each other's busy lives in one home. For most, then along come the children. So there is further need of refocused affections and nights with little sleep! There are the normal issues of finances, income, expenditure and what to sacrifice. There are important issues of communication, entertaining and hospitality. There are parents, yes and the in-laws! But this is what you got married for, despite it all, isn't it?

So, the two become one. But, as the old joke asks, 'Which one?' Yet another pressure...

Unfortunately a problem exists for today's married men, which didn't exist when I was younger. Research recently undertaken by BBC Radio 1's Newsbeat and the Portman Clinic has uncovered that 8 out of 10 men and 35 percent of women aged 18–24 have accessed pornography. And the average man in the UK spends over 2 hours a week looking for internet porn while women do so for 15 minutes. Alarmingly over half of men and a little under half of women disclosed that this 'in moderation' was fine. But 25 percent of men confessed they were worried about the amount of porn they viewed as well as the type of images. As Paul Woolley pointed out in *Christianity* magazine[1], this dehumanises human beings and breaks the intrinsic link between sex and a relationship.

A summer 2012 *Time* magazine article revealed that 76 percent of people aged 25–29 (the age of most people getting married) have used text messaging to flirt; 55 percent have sent suggestive pictures and 36 percent have co-ordinated committing adultery! We have the right to believe whatever we want, but not everything we believe is right!

Richard Stengel, Managing Editor of *Time* noted, 'The average smart phone today has more computing power than Apollo 11 did when it journeyed to the moon! So where will we be and what will we be able to do in 10 or 20 years time?'

Another world?

Finally there are issues young romantics never dream of. What affect will all the above have on children? In the West it is reckoned that the best age for children to start using mobiles is 13 years.

An NSPCC study discovered that a third of under-18s have been affected by 'sexting', and that it is not uncommon for girls as young as 11 to be asked to send intimate pictures to boys they know. They are also faced with a barrage of messages demanding intercourse or oral sex. Andy Phippen, Professor of Social Responsibility at Plymouth University says: 'The worrying thing is young people are starting to think this is completely normal.' He also commented on the fact that boys expect girls to behave in the same way they see women behaving online – and that girls believe they should live up to those messages.

In the summer of 2012 Dr William Struthers, a neuroscientist and academic, told MPs that children's first exposure to porn is so shocking that it becomes impossible to erase. He went on to explain that 'mirror neurons' in the brain makes young people more likely to act what they've seen out. He also said that porn is an 'accelerator', which makes young people have sex earlier. He continued speaking of a lost generation of boys who have problems forming attachments and who become increasingly isolated.

Suicide is the biggest killer of under 35s and dehumanising porn plays a role in that: we've already seen how close Nathan came to it as a result of his addiction.

Back to basics

As Christians we have to face the fact that there is ambivalence about marriage in society today, especially as 'moving in' is a cheaper and more immediate option.

But 2,000 years ago the academic Paul (formerly Saul) recalled, 'A man shall leave his father and mother and be united to his wife, and the two will become one flesh. This is a profound mystery'. (Ephesians 5:31–32) This mystery cannot work with two people of the same sex and rarely does between people who have made no public commitment to each other either.

New York Times bestseller Timothy Keller notes in his brilliant book, *The Meaning of Marriage*, that nothing can mature character like marriage. In it he also includes sociologist Linda J Waite's comment that 'the benefits of divorce have been oversold', adding that in the vast majority of cases divorce does not make people happier. Research also confirms that children who grow up in traditional married, two-parent families have two to three times more positive life outcomes than those who do not.

Legal scholar John Witte Jr is also quoted by Keller, and he comments that: 'marriage as a permanent contractual union designed for the sake of permanent love, procreation, and protection is slowly giving way to a new reality of marriage as a "terminal sexual contract" designed for the gratification of the individual parties.'

Keller also quotes Parker Pope: 'Marriage used to be a public institution for the common good. And now it is a private arrangement for the satisfaction of individuals. Marriage used to be about us, now it is about me.'

The New York Times writer Sara Lipton drew up a list of prominent married political men who refused to let marriage confine their sexual appetites and so cheated on their wives, children and friends.[2] These included Arnold Schwarzenegger, Dominique Strauss-Khan, Newt Gingrich and Bill Clinton. I could add to that list Prime Minister John Major (who later repented in shame and humility), Tiger Woods and more recently author and speaker, Mark Stibbe. The resulting pain, betrayal and loss are immeasurable.

Expectations

The use of porn also increases men's expectations of their wives and girlfriends, who are not porn stars. They have responsibilities, children, occasional sickness and real headaches! (Unlike the un-real porn stars.)

Porn is a totally unreal, non-relational world where many 'happy' stars live in appalling conditions under unbelievable threats.

It is an illusion that when we find 'the one' that everything damaged within us will be healed. There are things a lifelong partner can do to help us on our path towards wholeness. But there are other things that only Christ can do! It is also unwise to allow one partner to take the place of Christ in a married relationship and be relied upon in unhelpful ways.

It is also untrue that marriage is suffocating, oppressive and basically causes an unhappy state. I have been married for 45 years, and am made of the same stuff as you. There are always things to work through in any relationship, but we have each other, friends, scripture and the Holy Spirit to help us.

As far as I am able to say, the best and most comprehensive writings on the subject of marriage come from Timothy Keller, who has written many brilliant books including *The Meaning of Marriage* mentioned above. *Newsweek* named him 'A C.S. Lewis for the twenty-first century'. And for what it's worth I entirely agree – he is brilliant, lucid, readable and commonly sensible! If you have never heard of him or read his material do consider buying his book – you will thank us if you do!

Notes

1. *Christianity* magazine, July 2011.
2. *The New York Times*, 16 July 2011.

Chapter 9

Words of Incredible Hope

Thank God you are not on your own. Here are four more stories of those who have overcome their problems. We hope they will encourage, strengthen and bless you...

Joshua George

During my teenage years I found it difficult to be happy. Although I had known about God since a young age, I never experienced Him largely because I was deceived about who He was. I often burnt myself with candles and cut myself with anything I could find. This was my attempt at coping with what I grew to understand as depression. That really wasn't the worst of it either. My sleeping was intermittent, my eating poor and hence I lost a lot of weight. I would have episodes of constant irrationality of thought and no control of what I did with myself, occasionally hearing voices when alone. At the back end of this dark season, masturbation found me at around the age of 17. I say that it found me because I can never remember consciously trying to discover it; it just happened. Fortunately, I have remained a virgin because I want to keep myself for my future wife and I have never watched pornography. I already knew that women in the trade are treated horrifically and knew that Jesus Christ equated lusting to adultery so I didn't want to offend Him.

As time progressed I started to use masturbation as an antidote to feelings of depression. I began to read scientific articles and online public forums that would say 'masturbating multiple times a day is normal and healthy' in order to justify this practice. I would ignore the fact that it was becoming increasingly frequent and my control over it had completely dissipated. While I would mostly do it at home, I occasionally did it in public toilets. My habit had become an addiction, a crutch. I began to use it as a system for reward. The problem was that it was all contained inside of my head. Everything would be okay – in my eyes – if no one knew about it. As it became a daily practice, I began to entertain thoughts of women in my head, fantasising about having sex with them to fuel my addiction. It was no longer because I was depressed; I was now in bondage to it. It was then that I began to realise that my problem really was a problem.

As much as I wanted to be free, I couldn't bring myself to tell anyone I knew. I was known as a confident, competent and 'Christian' young man; I was afraid of that image changing. I feared man not God. What I didn't understand was that it was never because of my character, efforts or successes that I had ever achieved anything in the first place. This bondage didn't continue to exist because God was trying to teach me a lesson or because of the mistakes of others: it was my pride that was keep me locked up. Nobody comes to God by their own merit. It is the humble that He gives grace to. He is looking for people that know they need Him: He was looking for someone like me!

At the age of 18, I found healing through the ministry of a number of people and encounters with Holy Spirit: a real miracle (a story in itself)! But my problem of masturbation seemed to occur perpetually. I tried to break this stronghold of lust. I mean, I really tried. I worked hard at it. But it was only later I learnt that Jesus' approach to sin is more radical (and successful) than mine. He doesn't control or manage sin or even ask us to work really hard at stopping it; He just gets rid of it.

On the night of the 6 April 2012, at around 11:30pm, I was feeling down and for the first time I contemplated watching pornography. I had just opened an internet tab to search for some when (out of the blue) someone I had never spoken to before sent me a message. His name is Gerald Coates. This was the message:

Hi Joshua – not sure whether I know you – but have some words for you. You are a FB Friend!

God's hand is heavy upon you – you have never been able to get away. It is a miracle that you are still in the race – there have been many pulls and pressures few if any know about. But God never gets disillusioned with you – He never had any illusions in the first place!! Take time to reflect and let Him know your heart for now and the future.

Much love Gerald.

On that night (and many others), God had made it so difficult for me not to see that He was after me, that He wouldn't stop until He had won me out of darkness for Himself. Instead of doing what I had planned to do (and what I frequently did last thing at night) I went straight to bed with this word running through my mind. Without even trying, I found myself meditating on God's words about me instead of the impure thoughts that usually filled my mind. From that night in April there was an immediate and significant reduction in my sexual activity.

Later, Gerald told me that he was co-writing a book on sexual healing. Over the course of a few days, I told Gerald my story and he put me in touch with Nathan, who has since become a close friend of mine – as has Gerald. Nathan began to reveal the truth about who I really was because of Christ in me and me in Him. I can especially remember one night when I called Nathan up. That night he prayed in tongues with me for a sustained period of time. The Holy Spirit told me then that, 'What I've done for him [Nathan] I will do in you, tonight'. So, while weeping, I lay on the carpet of my room, completely broken, and I received what God had always had for me: Love. His mercy that He extended to me was greater than the sin I had committed against Him. God was better at being good than I had been at being evil. He was just so kind with me. It was after this night that the addiction of masturbation completely left me. I am now happily free! Yahoo!

I have learnt that people who seem to be 'all sorted out' just aren't and furthermore they are missing the point if that's how they try to appear. God sees our weakness as His chance to demonstrate His goodness. We don't repulse Him. We were made for each other. It is funny that it is the messed up people that go to God that are being perfected, not the perfected person who relies on himself. Pride opposes Him; humility attracts Him.

'So I'll gladly spend my time bragging about my weakness so that Christ's power can rest on me.' (2 Corinthians 12:9, CEB)

I am now happier than I ever have been, ever. I am living my dream by studying medicine at university. The battle had always been over my mind and more specifically my imagination. Now, I really do spend hours trying to fathom the depths of God's love for me. I spend time imagining what it would look like for God to turn up in a GP surgery or at football practice or a pub. Because Christ's power can now rest on me I am seeing miracles regularly, preaching the good news and simply enjoying myself! I now am awoken at night not because of nightmares, but because God wants to tell me how much He loves me. The night season is now God's stage not Satan's. I can't begin to describe how good God has been to me. I now live, free, to see Heaven on earth!

William

Life was busy growing up. I was being pulled between sport, music lessons and out of school tutors by my parents for the majority of my teens. Porn and wanking did not seem to be an issue because I didn't have time, at least I thought I didn't.

Once I had reached the age of 15, though, porn invaded my life through an older family friend who my parents trusted. It was a bizarre experience having vile images shoved in my face and not knowing what to do or think. At first I really did see the images as vile. My gut reaction was 'this does not seem right', but my curiosity grew so big it pushed my conscience out of the picture. For a while I was hooked, viewing porn twice a week for a sustained period of time.

At university procrastination seemed to go hand in hand with viewing porn in my first year. At this point I knew I had to take some radical steps, especially since I started to be involved in Christian leadership. In my third year a group of guys got together and began to talk openly about porn. We started to ask really tough questions of each other and talked honestly. It seemed that as soon as one person said they struggled with porn everyone in the room opened up to say they did. It became clear to me that God, through grace, does not take away the gifts He has bestowed upon us, but in fact is looking for us to be vulnerable with Him and with friends we trust.

During this period God's word, God's people and God's Sprit were prompting me to sort my life out and actually hate sin and stop pretending. This became very clear to me one day when I watched a video of an ex porn-star who had become a Christian. Suddenly porn didn't feel so detached. It struck me that porn stars are real people seeking real answers. How can we make Jesus the clear answer when we subscribe to the same lifestyle? Let me make it clear, though, that ridding yourself of the slavery of porn takes more than reading about a porn actress; it takes a move of God in your life. Grace is the most profound phenomenon you will ever encounter. When we live in grace we stop trying to look at porn in our own strength. Instead we start to be honest with God and tell Him our struggles as we ask Him to help us. Have you ever cried out to God when overwhelmed by the frustration of your sin?

Receiving God's grace is the most powerful weapon we can use against our addiction. However, there is some great practical advice that I am eternally thankfully for. For most guys the invention of the laptop and internet has made porn easy. My suggestion would be, if you are truly serious about giving up, leave the laptop at the bedroom door. For a lot of Christian guys the bedroom is the place where these issues take place. A wise person spoke into my life saying 'change what the bedroom is for': pick up a book, play some music, write a letter to a good friend, go old school for a while for the sake of being obedient to Jesus. I committed to having a bedroom free of my laptop for as long as it took. Scientists say it takes four to six weeks for habits to change. For me, after six weeks the laptop stopped being a temptation but I still do not leave it in my room.

A friend of mine took his desire to rid himself of porn seriously by linking his web history to his mother's email account. If he accessed a remotely unsavory website his mother would receive an email that week. I am not saying this is advice we should necessarily all subscribe to, but include it to highlight the extent to which people go to to change their habits. As Christians we should desire taking radical steps to deal with habitual sin in our lives.

Let me make it clear that you cannot have the practical without the spiritual. Without the focus of grace it is only a matter of time before you find loop holes in the rules you have set yourself. You will start to take bigger and bigger risks. You will start to thrive off the buzz of not being caught. The Proverbs writer drums this point home by saying: 'Whoever walks in integrity walks securely, but he who makes his ways crooked will be found out'. (Proverbs 10:9, ESV)

You might have heard the occasional preacher say, 'this is the generation that will change the world' or 'now is the time'. I do not dispute these claims but worry that hollow, weak Christians will never change the world for a moment. We need to get back to the heart of discipline and discipleship to change this world. Choose to pursue God – you *cannot* pursue both God and porn.

Ben Cooper

I heard people talking about it, and I was curious. After nothing happened I became worried and eventually I even feared that I was infertile. That's a strange fear to grip a 13-year-old boy.

One evening when I was 14 I 'successfully' masturbated for the first time while watching a seedy adult film on television. I was proud and felt that my manhood and fertility had been proven. Each time after that served as yet another affirmation of that fallacy. But, even back then, before I knew Jesus, it created a hollow feeling that I tried to ignore.

Things developed into an unhealthy interest. I started by looking through the TV guide and staying up late to watch any programme that might contain some illicit material. This affected my sleep and my ability to interact with my family during the day.

Meanwhile my discovery of the internet only served to increase my hunger for porn into a growing addiction. My taste soon moved from 18-rated movies to hard-core pornography – needless to say I was masturbating every time. I used to get annoyed when other siblings or my parents were in the house because I wanted to be alone with the computer. I even resented my dad coming home early from work because I knew he'd use the computer. My addiction was all-consuming.

It was never something I talked to other people about; it was always secret. I had no idea at the time that it was destroying my thought life and the way I interacted with women.

At the age of 16 Jesus found me. The hollow feeling increased into a godly sorrow. It affected me deeply but the addiction continued. Meanwhile I was fascinated by my new Saviour, who steadily began asking for more of my heart. But my addiction remained. I decided that after sixth form I would spend my gap year learning more about my faith.

Then one day I was simply sick and tired of being sick and tired. I couldn't face it anymore. And the porn just stopped.

I left for my gap year having been porn-free for a month. Naturally my desire to masturbate decreased, although it never ceased (and continued to be an on-off bi-monthly [rather than daily] struggle). I began to recognise times when I would be more prone to lust and learnt good habits that helped me resist. Having my alarm clock on top of my Bible and stopping the 'porn film in my head' were great ways of keeping my mind clean. I constantly asked for God's strength.

When I started university I had my own room, my own laptop and my own computer. Alarm bells rang. My heart was on fire for Jesus, I was in love with Him and knew He had my life. I didn't want porn back. So a few friends and I started a group called 'Fight Club'. It was a guys' accountability group. All you had to do to get in was tell the whole group the most shameful thing you had ever done – from there the only way was up. Fear of rejection keeps us in the dark. Vulnerability throws us at the mercy of His grace.

The very act of accountability, confession and prayer created an obvious freedom in our lives as we confessed things we'd been carrying for years. Meanwhile we served as support to one another in the area of being accountable over porn/masturbation. Anyone will find that having to tell up to eight people at the end of the week that you have been engaging with porn will seriously decrease your desire to do so!

The group meetings lasted for the duration of the first year at university.

By this point I was in a relationship, with the woman who was to become my wife, and our physical relationship steadily became a problem. It would seem that robust barriers against pornography and masturbation were not enough to stop us from being intimate to a degree much further than our relationship commitment deserved.

My biggest regret is that we never talked about our boundaries in the first few weeks of our relationship. I felt that it would be 'too awkward'. This cowardice paved the way for a steadily increasing physical relationship that we eventually both regretted. While it never led to intercourse, we owed one another a much higher standard of purity – so many things are worth protecting and saving until they can be enjoyed in the context of marriage.

Meanwhile I was still passionate for Jesus and excited to see people impacted by the gospel. But, as you can imagine, that conviction was threatened at times.

We felt so guilty that we sat another couple down who we were close to and told them everything. It just so happened that they were dealing with the same boundary issues and they confessed back to us! Again vulnerability and loving relationship opened the door to freedom.

Opening up to our friends broke the habit and things moved from a continuous desire to sporadic temptation – the habit had been broken and accountability, prayer and love helped all of us live the lives of purity we desired.

At one point in our relationship we even stopped kissing for a time. We found this reduced the expectancy of physical interaction and helped us maintain our boundaries.

At the very end of my time at university I went through a very stressful period of my life and felt the pull back to pornography. I was too embarrassed to tell my girlfriend or anyone else (after all I was the one who had helped people with their journey).

The addiction was not as strong as before – in quantity or explicitness – but it was there in the background. This included late nights looking at garbage and masturbating.

I eventually confessed to a friend and we supported one another but I should have also confided in my now wife.

It wasn't until six months before I was married that the habit ceased altogether. I found computer programs like X3 watch and Covenant Eyes to be extremely good (my advice would be to choose a local accountability partner you would *least* like to know about your internet activity). And simple habits like leaving my laptop in a housemate's room made things much easier at night.

Through cowardice it wasn't until after I was married that I told my wife about this period of my life. I seriously regret dragging the issue into our marriage.

I still don't take purity for granted and live life in accountable, loving and supportive relationship with those around me. My biggest desire is to stay vulnerable and be quick to confess. This journey has been one with more than its fair share of ups and downs but each time I've seen Jesus pull me through and my desire for a life of purity has increased.

Ben John

It was in year 8 when a friend of mine showed me some kind of adult content on his mobile phone. At the time I didn't really understand what it was all about, but it got me intrigued to find out more. Around the age of 13–14 hormones kicked in and through high school friends' conversations, I found out what the guy downstairs could do! So by the end of year 8 going into year 9 I was occasionally wanking but also still wanted to know more about the images my friend showed me on his phone.

It was at this time that I discovered what Google images had to offer. I first searched for what I thought was fairly innocent stuff. This continued throughout the whole of year 9, and I began searching more frequently and typing in more graphic words. I never even realised it at the time, but, by the end of year 9, I was using these images a fair few times a week (anything from a few times to every day of the week) for roughly 20–30 minutes to stimulate myself. This was always done on my parents' computer and I just learnt how to wipe the computer clean of history so that no one ever found out.

During year 10, the start of GCSEs, I bought myself my first computer. This was the true beginning of what started my addictions. Because I now had my own computer in the privacy of my own room I searched deeper into the web and went from Google images and erotic artwork websites to exclusively pornographic websites. I then went from just looking at pictures to watching videos and this snowballed into a strong addiction.

Towards the very end of year 11 (at the end of my GCSEs)

I gave my life to Christ at my local church, which I had been invited to. I then met a wonderful girl there who is still my girlfriend today. My life was going great, however no one knew about the addictions I was carrying. Before I had had a relationship with Jesus I didn't have the conviction from the Holy Spirit telling me to stop. I knew deep down from year 8 that what I was searching for on the internet wasn't exactly anything to be proud of, but now I knew I had a big problem that needed to be cut out.

Even though I tried to stop, the addictions carried on throughout A levels and into my first year at university. By this point I had told one of my youth leaders and a friend in my youth group who struggled with the same problem. Fortunately he managed to catch onto it far earlier than I did and took control. We decided to become accountable to each other and use X3 watch, which emails our internet histories to each other. This then brought an end to internet pornography on my computer. Well, until about two weeks later when I gave in and searched for the exact same content on my iPhone.

So it started all over again. I didn't even tell my youth leader or accountability partner. I was too ashamed. For about a month I was hooked onto my phone every night, for anywhere from 20 minutes up to two hours in one sitting, looking at porn. I couldn't get the images out of my head and I carried round the guilt all day. It had a massive effect on my image of myself. I hated myself. I clearly remember having a session on my iPhone then straight after it all just sitting on my bedroom floor in tears wondering if I was ever really going to be free and pleading with God to find me a way out. I was only 19 and I was completely addicted!

In the summer of 2012 the answer to many prayers was about to come! God had set me up for freedom. A guy who I didn't know at the time gave me a prophetic word. One of the key words he had was that I needed to build a firewall around myself, to protect me from worldly things. At first I had no idea what that meant. We talked a little on the phone for the next few days after he gave me the initial word. By this point I knew who I was speaking to – Gerald Coates. He started telling me about the book you're reading right now and I knew that the journey Nathan and Gerald were on would release me into freedom, because of his wisdom and Nathan's history.

Since the prophetic word, occasional phonecalls with Gerald and what God is doing in my heart, I am totally free from pornographic addictions and its sister every night. I've gone from being stuck to the stuff for hours every day to instant freedom and no porn in my life. Through this I have tasted God's grace like never before and I now know what it's like to walk in the true freedom that Jesus fully paid for. I just don't have to accommodate filth anymore. All glory to Him!

Chapter 10

Identity – Sexuality – Calling

So. What happens after you finish reading this book?

What we pray happens now – actually what we hope has already started – is that the teaching, stories and scripture take their effect. We pray that you will seize each piece of advice and practically apply it to your life. How you choose to receive what God says over you, has given to you and called you into, will determine if you can confidently state that you live under Christ-gained freedom.

The sister problems corrupt our understanding and applications of our identity, sexuality and calling, so here are some questions and statements of truth for you to work through.

Identity

Who do we say you are?
You are a child of the Creator of the universe, co-heir with Christ. You are *not* insignificant.

Who does God say you are?
You are incredibly loved individual who has been forgiven, set apart and made holy. You have purpose.

What are you defined by?
You are defined by Christ's death and resurrection, identified by who God says you are. You must never allow sin to define you. Sin is what you *do*, it is not who you *are*.

What do you live for?

You live to make His name known, to worship God in word and deed and live in His Kingdom with your thoughts and actions.

Sexuality

Is sexual sin worse than any other?
The wages of sin is death but the penalty for your sin has been paid for. You have not been partially set free, this is a *complete* salvation. The Cross was thorough!

What is the original intention?
The original purpose is for sex to take place between a man and a woman. So, single or married, you choose your behaviour and are responsible for it. You are better than a tenth-rate corruption of your sexuality through porn or masturbation.

Calling

What are you called to do?
You are called to be in relationship with God. You are set free to love God and others, living for Him above all else.

What prevents you from living out your calling?
No obstacle is greater than God's salvation for you. Sin puffs us up and diminishes God's power to bring change in our lives.

Conclusion

You have been chosen, you are important. Who you are being perfected into is vital in reaching this world with the message of God and His coming Kingdom. He has plans for your future and is faithful with His promises.

Remember and live out of the truth, live a holy life of freedom and actively speak victoriously over the devil's lies. You *can* embrace the freedom that God has provided.

Goodbye?...

You may never meet us, though we have received many invitations from youth organisations, church networks and cities to do seminars and public meetings specifically for guys. Do come and say 'Hi' if you attend one of these in the future.

We want to thank you for reading this book. We have never looked for platforms but we do want to help people like you.

We assure you of our continual prayers for those who have read this book.

Nathan and Gerald

Although Gerald and Nathan cannot enter into lengthy correspondence they would love to read short stories of breakthrough, deliverence and significant changes of behaviour. Any such stories may be posted on their website but without giving your full name! These stories will encourage others – they are important.

www.sexualhealingbook.com

You may like to consider asking Gerald and Nathan to a men's event in your town, city or youth organisation. They can also be contacted at PO Box 357, Leatherhead, Surrey KT22 2ED.

A significant part of the proceeds from this publication will be going to Gerald and Nathan's work in Uganda with pastors, churchplanters and schools with Gulu International Mission.